W9-BSV-666

Navigating the Nonsense

Navigating the Nonsense

CHURCH CONFLICT AND TRIANGULATION

DOUG BIXBY

Foreword by KAREN A. MCCLINTOCK

CASCADE *Books* • Eugene, Oregon

NAVIGATING THE NONSENSE
Church Conflict and Triangulation

Cascade Books
An Imprint of Wipf and Stock Publishers
199 W. 8th Ave., Suite 3
Eugene, OR 97401

www.wipfandstock.com

ISBN 13: 978-1-4982-2852-7

Cataloging-in-Publication data:

Doug Bixby.

Navigating the nonsense : church conflict and triangulation / Doug Bixby.

xxii + 104 p.; 23 cm—Includes bibliographical references.

ISBN 13: 978-1-4982-2852-7

1. Christian leadership. 2. Church work. 3. Pastoral theology. I. Title.

BV652.1 .B48 2016

Manufactured in the USA.

To my daughters Katie and Kiersten
For all the love, life, and laughter we share!

Contents

Foreword

IN DOUG BIXBY'S NEW book church leaders have a chance to take a look under the proverbial rug—where long buried secrets lay molding, and denied interpersonal conflicts threaten to trip up new members. When church lay leaders play emotionally shifting roles, clergy are often too close to the dynamics to see them clearly. Author and congregational consultant Doug Bixby trains readers to notice underlying emotional fields and provides ways to eliminate problems. Using this book, clergy and lay leaders can more effectively assess and change negative relational cycles.

I met the author when senior staff at the Alban Institute asked us to combine our experience for a clergy leadership seminar. Before agreeing, I read Doug's first book, *Challenging the Church Monster.* Upon finding his humility and insight quite astonishing, I said "yes" to our assignment. We provided a training program that helped clergy from multiple denominations create relationally healthy churches. Doug's respect for each person in the room became quickly evident and his ability to build confident leaders influenced each participant. As he had previously noted, "people are tired of churches that seem more focused on meetings than ministry and more focused on conflict than community." Doug Bixby provides the means to shift these dynamics by highlighting six levels of communication in *Navigating the Nonsense.*

Walking up toward a church I was visiting for the first time, I was overwhelmed by the enormity of its stone edifice, and the beautiful mahogany arched doors that opened to the sanctuary. Stained glass windows urged me to come in and see how they reflected the day's sunlight from the inside out. The greeters were friendly and didn't prod me for information or look askance at me. The pastor preached a solid sermon. At the offering time a mom with a baby asleep on her shoulder came by with a brass plate, and I was happy to see that the baby hadn't been whisked away to a cry room or a nursery so I could watch her peaceful face as she slept. The bulletin listed the week's programs, Bible study groups, volunteer opportunities, and the names of people to pray for. But throughout the morning I felt as if the congregation was in mourning for itself, with two thirds of their pews vacant. I couldn't help my distracted thinking about why this congregation wasn't thriving.

Reading Bixby's new book, readers will understand the complex dynamics that keep congregations such as this one from thriving. In his writing, biblical stories come alive with relevance for the congregations in our times. He names and addresses several chronic and possibly fatal relational diseases. Bixby's theories build upon and expand Stephen Karpman, MD's model of relational triangulation, applied by Murray Bowen, MD to family systems in the late sixties. The theory has also been used in church systems education by Peter Steinke at the Alban Institute. A new leader in this tradition, Bixby wisely says, "We need to talk *to* people, not *about* them."

Bixby's years as a senior pastor and church consultant have prepared him to draw upon a variety of experiences and theoretical models. He writes about church leadership with a pastor's heart from a pastor's study. He provides keen insights into the possible problems beneath the surface that lead to those empty pews. Doug's writing voice reflects the warmth and high regard he holds for clergy and laity who unconsciously engage in destructive patterns.

Now, let's take a look at a possible scenario at the stone church in the week ahead. On Monday morning, the choir director walks into the office and begins complaining to the church secretary about the people in his choir. On Tuesday two parishioners go to lunch with a new couple in the community and complain that the pastor doesn't make enough home visits. Later that week, someone on the personnel committee repeatedly releases confidential information about an employee. On Friday, a "well loved" former pastor goes on a hospital visit and promises the dying woman's family she'll conduct the funeral without the permission or blessing of the current pastor. That afternoon, the current pastor finishes up his sermon and leaves the office feeling overloaded and burnt out. He doesn't realize that his own conflict avoidance strategies are part of the problem.

Luckily, clergy can purchase and read *Navigating the Nonsense* before leaving their positions and laity can read it before locking the doors for the last time. Congregations can utilize this book to train their staff and laity to eliminate the dangerous dynamics just described. At that point—in gratitude to Bixby for their new insights—they can love one another as Christ's body in the world.

Foreword by Karen A. McClintock, MDiv, PhD, Author, Psychologist, and Congregational Consultant.
www.healthycongregation.com

Preface

MOST MINISTRIES ARE FILLED with significance and purpose, and they ought to bring meaning and satisfaction to those who are a part of it. The sad thing is that nonsense gets in the way. Conflict and controversy take hold of our relationships and limit our capacity to function and flourish. This leaves pastors feeling frustrated. It leaves church leaders overwhelmed and congregations disillusioned. This is why "navigating the nonsense" is so important. This book will help you to avoid these risks and pitfalls in ministry. It will help you to understand why this nonsense gets in the way and how you can avoid it. It will help clergy and their churches to enjoy their ministries and to increase their opportunities for making a significant difference.

Navigating the Nonsense is a part of all of our lives, our families, and our communities. We all live with a certain amount of conflict and controversy in our relationships. This can be particularly challenging in our churches where things can even be less predictable and under control. This is why many of us try to avoid conflict whenever possible. This conflict avoidance, at times, leads congregations into more chaos and confusion. The relationships in conflicted congregations seem fragile, at best. Very little true community exists within church systems where the nature of interpersonal interactions seem shallow and shortsighted. This lack of quality communication is above all else sad when the relationship between pastors and churches end prematurely. When this happens both clergy and congregations end up discouraged and depleted. My deep concern for pastors and churches is my primary source of motivation for writing this book.

When I was in seminary, no one ever told me that ministry would be easy, and yet it has been more challenging than I expected. At the same time it has been meaningful and significant. I feel blessed to have had the opportunity to serve God in this way. Navigating the nonsense has been a big part of my life. It has been a part of the challenge and satisfaction that I experience in ministry. Navigating the nonsense has allowed the ministries of the churches that I have served to have a bigger impact in the world. It has allowed people to experience God's grace, to learn from his Word, to share in supportive community, and to serve God by serving others. The church can be a beautiful place. I am not talking about the buildings, but the people. When our relationships are strong and people share in community with each other, God's glory can shine through our congregations. No churches are perfect, but they can be beautiful places where the glory of God can shine and Christ's joy can be experienced.

In John 15:11, Jesus said, "I have said these things to you so that my joy may be in you and your joy may be complete." This verse suggests that Jesus wants his disciples and his churches to be filled with joy. Not fake joy but real joy. With a little effort and intentionality, pastors and local church leaders can improve their communication patterns. This can help them to limit the impact that conflict and controversy on their congregations. There will be less drama and more meaningful ministry taking place. This book will help churches to establish more trust within their relationships and to experience Christian community on an entirely new level. This is not a book about simple solutions but, rather, it is a road map that can help direct your churches to function more appropriately and flourish more completely. It will be a guide that can help you to do the necessary hard work to keep conflict from taking over and chaos from overwhelming your church. It offers insight into the way churches work and how they can improve to fulfill their mission.

Acknowledgments

SINCE THE YEAR 2008, I have been serving as the Senior Pastor of the Evangelical Covenant Church in Attleboro, Massachusetts. Prior to that, I spent fifteen years as the Lead Pastor of Salem Covenant Church in Washington, Connecticut. This book is largely based on the experiences I have had with the people, staff, and organizational systems in both of these congregations. I am truly grateful for all who have helped to give shape to this book. In particular, I would like to thank the youth ministers, associate pastors, music directors, church secretaries, and my pre-school directors for all the life lessons and leadership challenges that we have shared in together. Special thanks to Chris Wall, Jay Fast, Cheryl Duerr, Julie Stevens, Carol Johnson, Robin Williams, Dina Spenciner, Linda Truffa, Susan Anthony-Klein, Andrew Newlin, Ben Zable, and Aaron Ruiz. You have all faithfully served with me, and I am grateful for all the things I have learned from you, for the friendships we have shared, and for the ministry we have participated in together. We have all collaborated in different ways and creatively served God in the roles that we have been in. Ministry is a team experience, and discovering the best ways to work together is what this book is all about.

I also thank friends who have helped. I am grateful to Karen McClintock for writing the foreword and for her support and friendship during this process. Whiney Hall is a colleague and friend who has graciously helped with reading and editing. Chris Wall, the Associate Pastor in Attleboro, has been an amazing support during the final steps in this process. Also, my friends Judy Peterson, Sarah Weaver, and Darrell Griffin have all helped in direct and indirect ways to give shape to the book. I am also grateful to the members of my pastor support groups. These groups have been a big part of my life during all these years in ministry.

I also extend my deepest appreciation to my family. My wife, Carolyn, is my greatest support. She is always my first and favorite editor, and she brings out the best in what I write and also in who I am. I am also grateful for the relationships I have with my daughters, Katie and Kiersten. They truly bring joy into my life, and I am proud of both of them on so many levels. They are smart, strong, beautiful, and talented young women. The relationships we share are truly a gift from God. The time we spend together are the most joy-filled times in my life. I am truly grateful for who you are and all that we share together.

Finally, I want to thank my editor at Cascade, Rodney Clapp. His expertise, encouragement, and editing have all been much appreciated.

Introduction

Many churches are closing their doors as a result of their failure to thrive in today's complex world. On the surface church conflict seems to be a strong contributing factor. However, conflict itself is not the problem. Conflict is a natural part of all human relationships and organizations. Some conflict even contributes to the health and vitality of our churches. The problem is the extent to which conflict takes a dominant role. Some churches experience so much conflict that it strangles them and stifles their ministries. Conflict at this level is distracting and destructive. It makes momentum and vitality in the church seem impossible. Too much conflict leads congregations into stagnation and, often, into a downward spiral. This is why we need to know how to "navigate the nonsense" within our ministries. In this book, I will reveal how direct communication helps congregations to rise above the conflict that is limiting the impact of their ministries and keeping them from moving into the highest levels of creativity and community.

Triangulation is the problem. Triangular relationships are relationships where at least three people interact with each other about one particular issue. Triangulation exists when one person is in the middle of what is going on between the other two. Sometimes these emotional triangles overlap each other and entangle a whole set of relationships. This ends up wasting a lot of the time and energy that could be invested in our ministries. One of the clearest ways to avoid emotional triangles is through direct communication. Direct communication is simply two people speaking directly to each other about one topic without attempting to draw others in. Pastors and other church leaders often get into trouble when they try to solve problems that exist between other people. Leaders also get into trouble when they seek to protect other leaders from conflicts. One way or another, we eventually discover that our place in the middle is hurting, not helping, as these emotional triangles get in the way. They waste the time, energy, talents, and financial resources of our congregations.

One reason the sitcom *Everybody Loves Raymond* is so funny is because of the number of relationship triangles created between all the family members in each episode. In one episode, Raymond's mother and father were in an argument. The mother and father took turns visiting with Raymond to talk about their marital issues. There was one point in the show when his mother was talking with Raymond about the trouble. Raymond shouted, "I do not want to get in the middle of this!" After a brief pause the mother responded, "Good, I don't want you in the middle. I want you on my side." This is triangulation. The problem with allowing triangles to form is that the parties involved always want you on their side, and when sides are created in the church, feuds develop. This is why direct communication is so important. This is why we must explore the best ways to navigate the nonsense in our relationships. The best thing Raymond could do for his parents was to stay out of the middle and to encourage them to talk directly with each other.

Conflict, compromise, cooperation, collaboration, creativity, and community are the six levels of communication in our churches. The communication in all of our churches includes each one of these levels of communication. However, the theory is that there is a tendency for all churches to hover between two of these levels, which I will call zones. The first zone I will write about hovers between "conflict" and "compromise." I call this the basement level of communication. Conflict is a common occurrence in these churches, and compromise is the primary way it is dealt with. Functional churches tend to hover between "cooperation" and "collaboration." This is the second zone. I call this level of communication the main floors. Churches that hover around the main floors work well together, and they lead their congregations into the higher elevations of communication. We can discover the highest level of communication in the higher elevations of "creativity" and "community." Zone III churches happily hover in a very positive atmosphere. They employ all levels of communication, but they hover in the realms of creativity and community.

Triangulation in churches has been addressed by a significant number of authors in a variety of church leadership books. I am indebted to these authors, and what I have learned from them. What I have noticed, however, is that triangulation is often treated passively as an inevitable part of our experience in the church. I have developed a strategy for minimizing church conflict by improving communication and avoiding triangulation. Triangulation is something that can be actively resisted by church leaders. Church conflict is inevitable, but triangulation is not. There are changes we can make to the way we relate to one another in the church to minimize the amount of triangulation that takes place. We cannot control everyone's behavior but we can control our own. Through this modeling we can teach our churches about how to communicate in appropriate ways. We can minimize the negative impact of triangulation and change the way we relate with one another in the church. This book will help pastors and church leaders to improve communication patterns and to experience the fruit of their labor.

The goal in all churches is obviously to experience as much collaboration, creativity, and community as possible. However, even in highly functioning churches it is imperative to understand how to "navigate the nonsense" on each level. This is why it is imperative that we understand the conflict, compromise, cooperation, and collaboration that needs to take place before we will experience these higher elevations. The best way to illustrate each level of communication is through stories. I will share stories that will help you to think through your own experiences. This book will help your church to develop a congregation-wide commitment to avoid triangular relationships. Such a commitment can help congregations to function better and to avoid toxic levels of conflict and intolerable webs of broken relationships.

If the concept of triangulation is new to you, this book will help you to understand it better. If you are familiar with triangulation, then this book will help you understand how a commitment to avoiding triangulation can help your congregation to keep conflict manageable and your mission in clear focus. All pastors and church leaders are responsible for providing momentum in their churches. One of the biggest challenges we face is the amount of conflict that interrupts and slows down our momentum. So the goal is not to get rid of conflict altogether, but to figure out ways to manage it and keep it at a healthy level. Some conflict is, in and of itself, healthy. It is a natural side effect of creativity. But, too much conflict can be destructive. This is why direct communication can help us. It can improve our relationships and maximize the amount of ministry taking place. This will help our churches to thrive.

Conflict levels also become unmanageable when there are major disagreements about who makes decisions. This is why effective church governance and leadership practices will help congregations to improve communication. At the end of each chapter, I will present a series of best practices for church leadership teams. These best practices will hopefully help your church to function better and create an environment that will help you to improve communication. This will not only help you and your church to understand the relationship between triangulation and conflict, but also to implement strategies that will help you to utilize direct communication more effectively. We all want to establish the kind of habits that will help our churches to enjoy the higher elevations of creativity and community.

Speaking of higher elevations, Jesus himself was a very direct communicator. Jesus' way of communicating did not allow him to enter into triangles. Jesus spoke directly to people, and he had a knack for getting out of emotional triangles. We will explore several of these stories in the Gospels. One example of this is in Matthew 19:13–15. In this passage, we hear the story about little children being brought to Jesus. It says,

> Then the little children were being brought to him in order that he might lay his hands on them and pray. The disciples spoke sternly to those who brought them; but Jesus said, "Let the little children come to me, and do not stop them; for it is to such as these that the kingdom of heaven belongs." And he laid his hands on them and went on his way.

Many of us refer to this passage as a way of understanding how Jesus related to children and how the church ought to treat children within the body of Christ. However, this passage also reveals something about how Jesus related to his disciples. Therefore, it also has something to say about how pastors and church leaders should relate to one another.

People were bringing children to Jesus. Then, the disciples got into the middle by trying to protect Jesus from them. This created a conflict between Jesus and his disciples. This happened because the disciples' interference was establishing a triangular relationship with Jesus and those who were bringing these children to him. When his disciples got in the middle, Jesus essentially says, "No, stop, don't do that." Literally, he says, "Let the children come to me, and do not stop them." Jesus was suggesting that they stay out of the middle and let him discern which boundaries he will set on his ministry. He did not want to limit the access of children to his ministry, and he confronted the disciples who tried to get in the middle of this, albeit with good intentions. The disciples were merely trying to keep others from taking advantage of Jesus. They were trying to draw a line to set boundaries. They were trying to protect him. However, Jesus knew that this boundary would send the wrong message to his followers about children.

This story illustrates how the disciples often got into trouble when they tried to protect Jesus. Jesus was not trying to embarrass his disciples, but the triangle they dragged him into established a teachable moment for all of his followers. Jesus wanted his disciples fully engaged with the mission that God had established for them, but he did not want them to get in the middle of his ministry relationships. In church settings, we often get into trouble when we try to protect one another from things we see as threatening. We need to understand that our place in the middle interferes with direct communication. It often makes challenging situations even more chaotic. In these situations, we are trying to help, but our helping actually ends up hurting. This is the problem with triangulation. Allowing triangulation to accumulate makes life within the church more complicated. It makes conflict more difficult to manage. The difference between conflict with or without an emotional triangle is the difference between a surface wound that can be easily treated and one that is allowed to fester and becomes infected.

This book has been written to help you to get out of the basement of communication and move up to the main floors so that your church can eventually experience the higher elevations on a more regular basis. Direct communication is the rich soil in which positive communication patterns can be cultivated. Avoiding triangles helps us to climb the ladder, moving from the basement of communication to the higher elevations. Each chapter of this book focuses on one rung of the communication ladder, starting with the bottom one. Through the practice of direction communication, we climb the communication ladder—moving up the ladder from conflict to compromise to cooperation to collaboration to creativity and, finally at the top, to community. When church people learn how to avoid emotional triangles, they learn how to communicate on a higher level. The spiritual and relational environment that is cultivated allows these churches to embrace better communication patterns. The fruit of improved communication patterns is the relationships that grow and flourish within our churches, the creativity that evolves, and the community that is experienced.

ZONE I: THE BASEMENT

The first two chapters of this book focus on the lowest level of communication. "Zone 1" churches are churches that hover between conflict and compromise. This is the basement. Sadly churches like this are consumed by conflict and overwhelmed by their problems. These congregations are in many ways addicted to conflict and feel like they cannot live without it. They feed on conflict and see it as a way of life. They see conflict as unavoidable, and yet they spend a lot of time and energy trying to manage it. Church members in these environments keep their distance from each other. They tiptoe around on eggshells, especially with people in leadership. Their relationships come across as fragile and futile. Compromise is seen as the only way of resolving conflict, and church leaders tend to see few other alternatives in the midst of their decision-making.

Some clear markers of a church stuck in the basement are the lack of communication between church leaders and the staff. There is also not enough communication among staff members and the church leaders themselves. The communication that does exist is riddled by a web of triangles, blame, and self-deception. There is very little trust. This is why the first zone is referred to as the basement of communication. All churches experience conflict and compromise, however, none of our churches have to hover in this zone. We will explore the significance of conflict and compromise in the first two chapters. In these first two chapters, I will show how triangulation and indirect communication keep us in the basement. The thread of hope, however, that runs throughout this book is that churches can get out of the basement and to spend as much time as possible in the higher elevations.

chapter 1

Conflict

As a lead pastor for over twenty years I have experienced church conflict in a variety of forms. I have experienced conflict over such things as the color of carpeting, the size of a refrigerator, levels of compensation, levels of staffing, the type of housing a church provides its pastor, the type of seating we provide for worship, the cost of a furnace, the type of stove we would use in the church kitchen, the type of music we sing in worship, Christmas decorations, the attire for the children's choir, the night of meetings, the time of meetings, worship schedules, program dates, and the groups we allow or do not allow to use our church building. All organizations, including churches, experience conflict. Conflict is simply a disagreement between two or more parties within a family, community, or organization. Indirect communication and triangulation are the two primary realities that allow manageable conflicts to escalate and become unmanageable. Some of the conflicts my churches have experienced have had to do with the budget and fiscal limitations; others were related to personal preferences; still others are related to mission objectives and priorities. However, in one way or another, all of these conflicts were manageable prior to the complications caused by triangulation.

Resolving conflict involves clearing up misunderstandings and reaching decisions in appropriate ways about important matters. This is where direct communication helps minimize conflicts. Triangulation tends to bring chaos and confusion into already complicated situations. A clear understanding of triangulation can help leaders to know how to navigate these complicated situations in ways that keep conflicts from escalating and taking on a life of their own. Encouraging direct communication is a powerful pathway to manage conflict and to keep it from taking control of our congregations. I have utilized this method of managing conflict for over twenty years, and it has served my congregations well. I hope this book will help you to see how your church can "navigate the nonsense" and improve your communication.

Triangles

When I was a child, my parents informed me that they were taking a trip to Bermuda. They were excited about their vacation, but all I could think about was the rumors I had heard regarding the Bermuda Triangle. The legend was that boats and planes often disappeared when they traveled through this imaginary Bermuda Triangle. My understanding was that there were more boat accidents and airplanes crashes in this area than any other place on the planet. So the last thing I wanted was for my parents to travel through it. I felt they should avoid this at all cost. As an adult, I would not hesitate taking a trip to Bermuda; I would actually welcome it. But I think that the church needs to avoid triangulation with the same amount of fervency that I once felt in relationship to the Bermuda Triangle. When we work hard to avoid triangulation in the church, we avoid both danger and disaster. I have seen way too many ministry ships go down and significant relationships crash as a result of these triangles that threaten our churches. These emotional triangles are real, and the stories are filled with pain.

I want to share a story with you about a church-related triangle I found myself in. Before I do I should give you a little information about myself and the church. I am the Senior Pastor of the Evangelical Covenant Church in Attleboro, Massachusetts. This is an active, established church in the southeastern part of Massachusetts. We have two services, as well as an active Sunday school and youth ministry. Our staff includes me, an Associate Pastor of Youth and Congregational Life, a full-time Director of Music Ministries, and a full-time Administrative Assistant. We have a part-time Sexton and a Director of our preschool and kindergarten. I came to Attleboro in 2008 from Connecticut. I served Salem Covenant Church in Washington, Connecticut for fifteen years. One of the things I clearly learned about triangulation at both of these churches is that there are often good intentions behind the behavior that leads into these emotional triangles. Often the person who creates the triangle is trying to help, not hurt, and this can make "navigating the nonsense" rather challenging.

My good friend D. Darrell Griffin, the Senior Pastor of Oakdale Covenant Church in Chicago tells me that his grandmother used to say, "No one likes change, except a wet baby." One of the things that was hard for me when I first arrived in Attleboro was making adjustments to a new way of doing things. I was used to doing things one way and they were used to doing them another way. It was hard to keep myself from changing too many things all at once. On a theoretical level, I knew that too much change all at once was not good for momentum. Despite this, I probably changed too much at first, and this amount of change made some people uncomfortable. There was one disgruntled member of the church who went into my associate pastor's office during the first few months of my tenure to talk about the amount of change taking place. The ironic thing is that she was the last person I would have expected to be uncomfortable with change. She had an adventurous spirit and a high level of energy. So her frustration surprised me. Nevertheless, she went into his office and shared her feelings with him. This pastor and I had already talked about triangulation in staff meetings, and he was excited to apply this theory. He saw this as a prime opportunity to encourage her to share these feelings directly with me, and this is what he did. She informed him that she would talk with me. This made him feel good because it took him out of the middle. So far, so good. But then Jay did something he should not have. He came to me and shared the story about his experience with this woman. This put him back in the middle.

Pastor Jay went on to tell me what she said to him in his office. He did this because he was trying to protect me. He was warning me about the conflict. He was giving me advanced notice. When he did this, however, he connected the dots and completed the triangle. The problem is that this emotional triangle created a significant amount of anxiety in me. I did not sleep well for the next several nights. Actually the person in question never came to speak to me. Apparently, she just needed to let off some steam by sharing her feelings with Jay. Talking with him was her outlet. The triangle would not have been formed if Jay did not tell me about the conversation. He completed the triangle and this created an unnecessary level of anxiety in me. I simply lost sleep, but when triangles like this start to pile up in our relationships, so do the consequences. Mistrust is a slow-growing cancer. The point is that Jay was trying to help, but it ended up hurting. The phrase "lose lips sink ships" comes to mind when I think about these issues.

The worst case scenario, if Jay had not come to warn me about this woman, is that I would have had a difficult conversation with her. I clearly did not need protection from this. As church leaders, we need to allow confidential space for people to share difficult feelings about issues in the church. It is good for people to express their emotions when they experience change and, sometimes, this is all they need to do. In many cases, leaders help simply by listening. When I first arrived in Attleboro, I quickly realized how supportive Jay was of me, and I wanted him to feel my support, as well. We saw this experience of triangulation as a case study, and we learned from it. I am convinced that our relationship became stronger because of the amount of time and energy we spent talking about the ways we should manage information and encourage direct communication.

Pastors and leaders at times need to resist the temptation to protect others if it means forming an emotional triangle. In his book *A Failure of Nerve*, Edwin Friedman writes,

> For leaders, the capacity to understand and think in terms of emotional triangles can be the key to their stress, their health, their effectiveness, and their relational binds. Almost every issue of leadership and the difficulties that accompany it can be framed in terms of emotional triangles, including motivation, clarity, decision making, resistance to change, imaginative gridlock, and a failure of nerve.[1]

This associate pastor stayed at our church for ten years. During his tenure, we spent a lot of time talking about triangulation so that we could protect our personal relationship and the relationships we had with members of our congregation. I had a great working relationship with Jay. The chemistry between us was good and our trust level was high. He is now the Lead Pastor at a church in Michigan. Avoiding triangulation helped us both to develop relationally and vocationally.

Helping

Trusting that other people can emotionally handle difficult conversations is one of the keys to avoiding emotional triangles. This is true for pastors and lay leaders. One of my first experiences with triangulation was an eye-opening experience for me. It took place when I was a student at North Park Theological Seminary. I was working as a Residence Hall Director at North Park University, which is a Christian college on the same campus as

1. Friedman, *Failure of Nerve*, 206.

the seminary. My boss was the Dean of Students, and I was supervising several Resident Assistants. These RAs were student supervisors who lived on each floor of the residence hall. They were responsible for helping students get settled into residence life, developing a sense of community on their floors, and making sure the students followed school policies. If a resident on the floor broke a school rule, then the RA would write that student up on a form and turn it in to me. I would then typically pass it on to the Dean of Students. The Dean would call the student into his office and manage the discipline process.

One of the school policies was no alcohol on campus. On this particular occasion, one of my RAs had to write someone up for breaking this rule. She arrived in my office with tears streaming down her face. She was very upset about this experience because it was one of her friends who broke the rule. This friend did not show a lot of respect during the confrontation. These confrontations were never easy. However, teaching young people how to confront was one of the meaningful aspects of this job. The write-up was eventually turned into the Dean of Students, and the violator was called into his office. The Dean chose to be lenient with this young woman and did not fine her or give her any real punishment. The person who received this leniency posted the letter on the door of her dorm room and laughed at the RA because nothing really happened to her. She rejoiced in the hand slapping she received.

The RA returned to my office with a new set of tears streaming down her face. She was obviously upset because of the Dean's lack of action. The RA did not feel supported by the Dean. I, then, did the right thing. I encouraged her to go and speak directly with the Dean of Students. I said he would probably learn something from the conversation. She quickly agreed and was glad I suggested it. She was going to set up an appointment with the Dean later that day, but I did something that interfered with this process. I bumped into the Dean later that afternoon in the center of campus. I went against my instincts and told him the story about her experience thinking it might prepare him for the conversation he would inevitably have. I was essentially trying to protect him from the difficult discussion with the RA. However, he did not respond well. He was very upset when I told him about this. He said, "I cannot believe that she did not come to me." I quickly realized I had formed a triangle with my RA and the Dean of Students. I tried to backtrack, but the damage was already done. My actions made this difficult discussion even more difficult and complicated.

If I had stayed out of the middle of this situation, then the RA would have gone to talk with the Dean directly, and I think both of them would have benefited from the conversation. When I got in the middle, I created an undue level of anxiety for the Dean, and this did not have a positive impact on his relationship with the Resident Assistant. I was trying to help, but it ended up hurting. My involvement in this triangle threatened their relationship. This is why avoiding triangular relationships is so important. To confess, I was not only trying to help, I was also trying to appear helpful to my boss. The truth is that I should have allowed these two to have this difficult discussion on their own. They could have handled it, and they would have been better off if I had not gotten involved. I should have avoided the temptation to appear helpful. Avoiding this temptation to give advanced warning will keep us from hurting the ones we are trying to help. Staying out of the middle in these situations enables others to work out whatever they need to work out on their own, in a less complex environment.

Entrapment

A classic story about Jesus being led into the middle of a triangle is the one about the woman who was caught in adultery. The example Jesus set for us in this situation is nothing short of brilliant—it was also beautiful. He utilized wisdom as a pathway for detangling a triangle that had been formed intentionally and maliciously. In John 8:3–11, it says,

> The scribes and the Pharisees brought a woman who had been caught in adultery; and making her stand before all of them, they said to him, "Teacher this woman was caught in the very act of committing adultery. Now in the law Moses commanded us to stone such women. Now what do you say?" They said this to test him, so that they might have some charge to bring against him. Jesus bent down and wrote with his finger on the ground. When they kept on questioning him, he straightened up and said to them, "Let anyone among you who is without sin be the first to throw a stone at her." And once again he bent down and wrote on the ground. When they heard it, they went away, one by one, beginning with the elders; and Jesus was left alone with the woman standing before him. Jesus straightened up and said to her, "Woman, where are they? Has no one condemned you?" She said, "No one, sir." And Jesus said, "Neither do I condemn you. Go your way, and from now on do not sin again."

This woman was objectified and used as bait in an attempt by the scribes and Pharisees to entrap Jesus. They used her to form a very intense emotional triangle with Jesus. If Jesus said or did the wrong thing, they would use this against him. This is why he wrote in the sand to delay his response, and it is the reason he made the statement that he made. He said, "Let anyone among you who is without sin be the first to throw a stone at her." This was his way out of the triangle, and it was the only way he could keep her from being objectified and used as a pawn in their attempt to entrap him.

Jesus' patience and thoughtfulness extricated the woman caught in adultery from the triangle she was forced into. This gave her a pathway out of the middle of the conflict Jesus was in with the scribes and Pharisees. Some of the conflicts we experience are between individuals. Many, however, are between groups of people or, as it was in this case, between an individual and a group. In this case, the real conflict was between the Pharisees and Jesus. This was why they were testing him. They were using this woman in an attempt to manipulate Jesus into saying or doing something that would get him into more trouble with their group. It was the wisdom of Jesus that allowed him to avoid the triangle and to protect the woman. In the end, he emphasizes that they did not condemn her. He sends her off and says, "Do not sin again." He was able to keep the situation from escalating without condoning her behavior. In the end he communicates directly with her in a redemptive way.

Mistrust

Mistrust can be devastating to our ministries. This is why establishing trust needs to be the primary goal in this first stage of any ministry. I like to refer to the first three years of any ministry as the "trust verses mistrust" stage. I am of course borrowing this phrase from the first stage of Erik H. Erikson's stages of human development.[2] I am convinced that "Trust versus mistrust" is the first stage in the development of a relationship between a pastor and his or her congregation. This idea is largely based on the experience I have had in these first three years of my ministries combined with my observations of other clergy and their churches. Some of the hardest conflict situations I have experienced in ministry arose in my first three years at both of my churches. I have also observed several of my colleagues who have experienced conflict on such a high level in their first three years

2. Papalia and Olds, *Human Development*, 145.

of ministry. Some of these situation have led to the premature end of their ministries. These are sad and difficult experiences for both clergy and churches. Often our expectations of new clergy or new congregations are too high, and disappointments in the first three years can have a dramatic impact on the relationship that is developing. These premature endings are emotional experiences for everyone involved, and they can leave both pastors and congregations feeling depleted. Triangles often run rampant in these kinds of complicated situations. This is why I am convinced that in this early stage churches and pastors need to be especially deliberate about "navigating the nonsense."

I am mindful of two of my colleagues who were called to serve their dream churches, and they ended up experiencing nightmares. These nightmare experiences took place in the first three years. In some ways the so-called "honeymoon phase" of a pastor's ministry is filled with vulnerability. The risks seem particularly high in churches with historic success and strong reputations. Nothing is more deadly for established churches than nostalgia or the heightened sense of entitlement that can grow out of a glorified past. Most high-steeple churches in mainline denominations have a glorified past that seems to hurt their present ministries. This not only leads churches to have unrealistic expectations of their clergy, but also for clergy to have unrealistic expectations of these churches. This is why Eugene Peterson writes these shocking words:

> Parish glamorization is ecclesiastical pornography (skillfully airbrushed) or drawing pictures of congregations that are without spot or wrinkle, the shapes that a few parishes have for a few short years. These provocatively posed pictures are devoid of personal relationships. The pictures excite a lust for domination, for gratification, for uninvolved and impersonal spirituality.[3]

One interim pastor in a Presbyterian church told me that he had just been called to his "dream church." However, it only took him a week to realize his parishioners were human and that they were not going to live up to the expectations he had of them.

The risks associated with the "trust verses mistrust" stage are particularly high when both the clergy and the congregation have unrealistic expectations of each other. It is possible for churches to airbrush and glamorize their new pastors in the same way that pastors can airbrush and glamorize their new churches. These unrealistic expectations often lead

3. Peterson, *Unpredictable Plant*, 22.

into a lack of patience with regard to the relationship-building process. I have also noticed that this trust-building process can be especially difficult for a new pastor in a church that had a relationship with the previous pastor end prematurely or for a pastor who experienced a premature ending in his previous location. Building relationships and developing trust is a delicate matter, especially during the first three years.

When I candidated at the Evangelical Covenant Church in Attleboro, one of the things I promised the congregation was that I would disappoint them. I said that no pastor is perfect, and that pastors inevitably end up disappointing people in their congregations. I said all this intentionally because I wanted the people of this church to keep their expectations of me in perspective. When expectations are too high for a pastor or a congregation, then the discovery of imperfections can lead into difficult levels of disappointment for everyone. My aim would clearly not be to disappoint them. However, I learned a long time ago that my aim needs to be to please God, not people. Pleasing everyone is not possible, and pleasing God becomes more probable when we are focused on his expectations. The amazing thing is that they still called me to be their pastor after I promised that I would disappoint them. I think they knew I would be honest.

One pastor I was coaching shared a story with me about a conflict in his church where the person in question ended up leaving the church. He tried to resolve the issues in a variety of different ways, but the person who left the church never returned. This was hard because this disgruntled member had several adult siblings still actively involved in the church. The interesting thing is that the siblings were not surprised that their brother had left the church. This brother had apparently left the church before, and it almost seemed like they expected it to happen again. They, however, did not want to be in the middle of the conflict. This pastor learned to respect this fact and kept the conflict between himself and the person who was upset with him. He did not drag the siblings into the middle of it. This actually helped him to keep the conflict isolated and benign. It did not spread or escalate. It stayed an issue between him and this person, and it did not have much of an impact on the church as a whole. Avoiding triangulation helps you to keep conflicts isolated between you and the individuals with whom you have the problem.

I have also discovered that serious chaos develops when you confront someone publically instead of privately. One way to avoid a web of triangles is to keep your difficult discussions between yourself and the person you have a problem with. When you begin talking about specific concerns with those not directly involved with the issues you inadvertently spin your own web. This is especially true if you talk with others as a way of avoiding the direct conversations you need to have. The primary point being we need to talk to people, not about them. When we talk about people instead of to them we leave the door wide open for triangulation. When someone stops attending your church the temptation is to talk about them instead of to them. On one occasion I remember calling a family that stopped coming to my church in Connecticut. I heard rumors that they were attending another church in a nearby town. My assumption was that a conversation would simply close the door on our relationship. When I called them they surprisingly asked if it was okay to come back. They felt bad about leaving and needed permission to return. This is a good example of how talking to people works better than talking about them.

Amplification

Peter Steinke says all conflicts need a "generator" and an "amplifier." He writes, "For any conflict to continue and to get out of control, a generator of anxiety and an amplifier are needed. They feed on each other."[4] The sad thing is that a pastor can inadvertently play the role of amplifier. We become amplifiers when we talk about people instead of to people. We take the conflicts other people generate and inadvertently spread them. Sometimes we do this because of our own anticipatory anxiety about the situation. We talk about the generator because we think it might help to protect us if the conflict is amplified. Ironically, this itself ends up amplifying the conflict. We strive to develop a few allies on our side of the situation before things get elevated, but it is this behavior that elevates the conflict. We inadvertently drag these other people into the middle. Conflict typically only needs two people, but amplification needs many more. So, if we seek to keep others out of the middle, then we can keep the conflict from growing out of control. If we avoid triangulation, we avoid amplification. Most generated conflict is manageable. Conflicts only become unmanageable when they are amplified by the indirect communication of those involved. The sad thing is that we are just adding fuel to a what would otherwise be a benign fire.

4. Steinke, *Congregational Leadership in Anxious Times*, 110.

One time I found myself in the middle of a triangle at a grocery store. I was waiting in a long line hoping they would open another lane. This is exactly what happened. The person in front of me in the original line had a lot of items in their cart, and I had a significant number of items in mine. When the new line opened I was instructed to move over to the new line. Then I noticed the person behind me only had a few items. I suggested that he go in front of me, and he accepted my offer with gratitude. A few moments later the original cashier saw that I was not in the front of this new line. She sought to protect me by telling the other person that I was entitled to this position in the line because I was officially "the next person in line." I tried to inform her that he did not infringe upon my rights as the next person in line. I gave him permission to go ahead of me. This conflict escalated, however, when the person in front of me felt offended by the cashier's involvement and started yelling back at her. From this point on I simply stayed out of the middle. The cashier was trying to help me in this situation, but there really was no conflict. There was, however, a triangle. I clearly did not need her protection, nor did she need mine.

There are times when we need to stand up for people who cannot stand up for themselves, but generally speaking we also need to learn how to stay out of the middle of most situations. We need to let the other adults around us stick up for themselves. If this much conflict erupted from a mix-up at the grocery store, then it should not surprise us that conflicts escalate within our congregations. It is also important to see that some of the people who cause triangulation are simply trying to help. This is not about bad people, but rather poor communication patterns. The cashier at this store was simply trying to protect my rights as "the next person in line." What she did not know was that I had given permission for this other person to go ahead of me. Sometimes it is the information we do not have that makes diving into the middle of a situation even more inappropriate. This cashier was merely trying to help, but she ended up offending an innocent person, who reacted harshly toward her. Once this conflict erupted, I simply tried to get out of the middle, because I knew that my place in the middle would make things even more complicated by compounding them.

The reason many of us are weary of conflict in our churches is because of the dominant role that it plays. Churches often develop significant patterns of indirect communication. The anxiety within systems like this helps to shape a culture that allows people to talk freely about others. We need to develop church cultures that encourage people to talk directly to others.

Indirect communication is the reason why some churches act like conflict is always bad. These churches tend to think that the best way to deal with conflict is to avoid it at all cost. The problem with avoiding conflict is that it keeps us from dealing with the real issues. We often encounter difficult situations that demand that we have difficult discussions. Sadly, many of us avoid these difficult discussions about real issues because we are afraid of generating a conflict. What we need to avoid is talking about others in ways that lead into amplification. When we have difficult discussions this helps us to avoid triangulation because we are talking *to* people, not *about* them.

Disagreements

Music ministry is one of the most challenging areas of church life for which we must "navigate the nonsense." The diversity of preferences and music groups in the church can lead to a lot of triangulation. The goal in all of this is not to avoid conflict, but triangles. I say this because there is no problem with having different opinions about specific matters. Problems arise when we allow these differences to interfere with our relationships. This often happens when conflicts get mixed together with triangular relationships. It happens when we stop speaking directly to each other. Triangles can have a negative impact on our ability to function as leaders. Triangulation allows minor conflicts to escalate faster than major conflicts that are contained between two people. The Director of Music Ministries at my church is a woman named Cheryl. Cheryl says that she is intentional about "falling into her problems." She actually dives right into them. She clearly does not avoid them. She is fearless about having difficult discussions. This has helped her to navigate the nonsense in our church. She knows that it is better to talk things out than it is to let them fester.

I was once working with a newlywed couple raising a child together. I met with the mother and the stepfather in my office. In this family situation, the mother was not allowing the stepfather to be fully involved in the parenting. She was not trying to exclude him from the joys of parenting, but she was trying to protect him from the challenges. She was trying to keep him from having to deal with discipline. If her ten-year-old son failed to do the dishes, then the stepfather would offer direction. In response the child would yell back at him, and the mother would jump into the argument to protect her husband and keep him out of the difficult discussion. She was trying to help, but this was actually creating a triangle between herself, her husband, and the child. This triangulation made all their relationships more difficult. We talked about triangulation, and I encouraged the mother to stop trying to protect her husband. She needed to stay out of the middle of their conversations, even when disagreements emerged. They have since informed me that this simple change in their family system transformed the way they were communicating. Imagine how this simple change could have long-term ramifications for this family for years to come. Then imagine how simple changes like these, in the relationships we have with people in our congregation, might impact our churches and ministries for years to come.

More often than not, difficult conversations seem to clear things up or, at least, reveal what the true issues are. In Matthew 5:23–24 Jesus teaches us about the importance of having difficult discussions. He says, "So when you are offering your gift at the altar, if you remember that your brother or sister has something against you, leave your gift there before the altar and go; first to be reconciled to your brother or sister." Conflict has a way of getting in the way of mission and ministry. There are always going to be issues and challenges within our lives and relationships. Churches are made up of people and relationships. This is why we must "navigate the nonsense" effectively. In 1 Corinthians 1:10 the Apostle Paul writes, "Now I appeal to you, brothers and sisters, by the name of our Lord Jesus Christ, that all of you be in agreement and that there be no divisions among you, but that you be united in the same mind and same purpose." This was clearly a lofty goal, but the goal emerged as a result of some of the first experiences people had with church conflicts. We all have differences and unique preferences and personalities that make achieving the biblical goal of "no divisions" difficult. Conflicts are simply disagreements, and these should not surprise us in a world as complex and diverse as ours. The good news, however, is that direct communication keeps the impact of conflict at a healthy level. Direct communication keeps conflict contained and tension from rising to toxic levels.

I once heard someone say that pastors should take a Hippocratic Oath like doctors do. The abbreviated version of the Hippocratic Oath is "I will do no harm." The opposite of doing harm is obviously offering help, and almost all pastors enter into the ministry to help, not hurt. The challenge we face in the church is that sometimes our attempts to help can end up hurting because of triangulation. In the church, we get in the middle of conflicts. Sometimes we are even dragged into the middle of them, and we are asked to take sides. Running away from problems does not help you to deal with them. This is why pastors, staff, church leaders, and church members all need to be committed to the churches' version of the Hippocratic Oath. We all need to be mutually committed to the goal of doing no harm. At the same time we need to recognize that none of us or our relationships will ever be perfect. There is always some pain in all relationships, and none of us can be held entirely responsible for all the pain that exists within any of them. We need to work at this together in our churches.

Some conflicted churches are notorious for allowing conflicts to spread into church parking lots and onto social networking sites. We often avoid conflict because we are afraid that disagreements will go viral, so we avoid talking about the issues in the first place. There is no such thing as a church that can avoid conflict all together. We all have it, and we all have to learn how to live with it. Avoiding difficult conversations can lead to deep divisions, and this can keep us from being "united in the same mind and purpose." In some ways, direct communication is the difference between having a disagreement and being disagreeable. It keeps conflicts from developing into divisions. When we deal with things as directly as we possibly can, problems get solved and issues get resolved.

We need to navigate the nonsense in our churches in much the same way that most of us have learned to do so in our families—very carefully! Most of us tend to accept the reality of conflict in our families better than we do in our churches. We are also more committed to working through the issues that arise in our families because we know that our relatives are still going to be our relatives after the argument is finished. Most of us also know that real divisions become deeper when other people get involved. If someone is offended by something a family member said, then it is far more productive to talk directly with them about the situation. It does not help if you take the issues to the family reunion and start speaking about them. We avoid this because we know what happens when we get everyone else in the family involved. We know it is better to have a small battle with one person than it is to create a war with a lot of other people. Including various others in our conflicts can turn small disagreements into full-blown battles.

BEST PRACTICE #1

The Pastoral Relations Committee

Pastoral Relations Committees are intended to help pastors and congregations to have a positive and productive relationship. These committees are sometimes called Mutual Ministry Committees or Personnel Committees. The goal of the Pastoral Relations Committee is to help strengthen relationships. The problem is that they often get caught in the middle of relationships, and they intensify conflicts that already exist. In some ways, these committees can be breeding grounds for triangulation. One chairperson of a Pastoral Relations Committee in her church recently contacted me. She informed me that their church has a new pastor, and the transition has been difficult. She is overwhelmed because most people in her church see her as the one who receives complaints and shares them anonymously with the new pastor. You can see that this is an intentional and institutionalized form of perpetuating triangulation. If she receives a complaint and shares it anonymously with the pastor, then there is no way for the pastor to process the issue with the person in question. If the identity of the person complaining is revealed, then that person who complained will most likely be upset with this chairperson. It is a no-win situation, and the only way to change the situation is to take triangulation out of the job description for the chair of this committee in the church.

Many churches give up on the idea of a Pastoral Relations Committee because of the dysfunction that typically evolves out of this type of interaction. Sometimes churches employ a Pastoral Relations Committee during the first few years of a pastor's tenure, and then they give up on the idea if the clergy person survives the "trust verses mistrust stage." In many ways, it is better not to have a Pastoral Relations Committee if they are merely serving as a breeding ground for triangles. Nevertheless, there are ways a Pastoral Relations Committee can effectively serve the church and its clergy. I think the best way for such a committee to serve is to give direct and honest feedback to the clergy about the ministries. Most pastors welcome this kind of input if it is coming directly from people who are willing to sit face-to-face and share it. It may seem easier for lay people to sit in a room and say that someone else raised a concern about something, but because of triangulation, this tends not to be very productive. When someone is invited to share both positive and negative feedback directly out of concern for the ministry, then this can lead into high levels of productive conversation.

The goal should always be improvement in the ministries, not perfection in the church. The goal needs to be progress, not perfection. There is no such thing as a perfect pastor or perfect church. There is also no such thing as a perfect relationship between a pastor and a congregation. Acknowledging this will help your committee to function at an optimal level. A Pastoral Relations Committee can also help to facilitate discussion between disgruntled church members and the pastor. If a conflict arises for someone, and they feel uncomfortable talking with the pastor alone, then a PRC member can offer to facilitate a conversation between the church member and the pastor. The role of the PRC member would simply be to initiate the conversation and to ask appropriate questions to open the dialogue. The key is asking questions and not giving opinions. Their role in this situation is to facilitate a conversation, not to act as a judge. Many of the conflicts that arise in churches are related to misunderstandings. Misunderstandings often clear up when difficult discussions take place.

The Pastoral Relations Committee as a whole can also help to navigate a difficult discussion and play the role of facilitator. In this case the PRC can invite the two parties to a meeting with the group. Then during the meeting, the PRC members facilitate the discussion with the aim of reconciling the relationship. The chairperson begins the discussion, but any PRC member can ask questions to increase the communication. The committee members must refrain from stating their opinions about the conflict situation. This allows the communication to essentially be between the pastor and the parishioner. In these situations it is the role of the chair to make sure the committee follows these instructions. This keeps PRC members out of the middle. The goal of all of such meetings is always reconciliation or to have the two parties come to a clearer understanding of their difficulties and each other.

If there is a clear accusation of a violation of pastoral ethics or parishioner ethics, then most denominations have a system for dealing with such matters. In these cases, the PRC should refer this issue to the church chairperson, and this person should ask for intervention or guidance from the judicatory (i.e., Bishop, Area Minister, or Conference Superintendent). Sometimes these matters are simply accusations, but when pastoral positions and ministerial standing are at stake, it is important to handle these situations appropriately. Issues like sexual misconduct, physical abuse, or financial infractions are not just a matter of interpersonal relationships, but pastoral integrity and the integrity of the pastoral office. This is why congregations with denominational systems are wise to refer these matters to the larger body. The members of a church may not always like the outcomes, but they will recognize the need for following proper procedures and respecting authority on these matters.

chapter 2

Compromise

One way to resolve a conflict is to compromise. Compromise is an agreement reached by two parties or groups of people who disagree about something. If the church staff enjoys having summer worship at 9 AM, but their Deacon Board is suggesting that summer worship start at 10 AM, then a 9:30 AM start would be a clear compromise. This is a situation where both parties give up something in order to reach a point of resolution. They meet in the middle. Compromise is sometimes necessary when both parties have a stake in a particular matter. If compromise is the most common way you resolve conflict in your working relationships, then more productive ways of seeking resolution ought to be explored. There is nothing wrong with compromise in and of itself. Even in churches where cooperation and collaboration are taking place, there are occasions when compromise is necessary. Challenging issues arise on occasion, however, if compromise is your primary way of resolving disputes. When compromise is seen as the only option, no one ends up feeling great about the outcomes. If this is the case, your communication patterns may continue to disintegrate. If your communication commonly hovers between conflict and compromise, then there will not be much joy within your ministries. This will lead your congregation to feel like it is locked in the communication basement.

Meetings

I once had the privilege of presenting several workshops at the General Synod of the United Church of Christ where the denomination celebrated fifty years of ministry. I presented these workshops for the Pilgrim Press on topics selected from my first book, *Challenging the Church Monster*. I spoke about moving our congregational focus "from meetings to ministry." Too often in our complicated church systems, meetings become the focal point in place of ministry. One of the ministers in my workshop shared a story with me. He said that his fourth-grade son was in school, and the teacher asked him what his parents did for a living. Instead of saying that his father was a minister, he said, "My father goes to meetings." One of the reasons it is essential for us to navigate the nonsense more effectively is so that we can shift our focus. All churches need administration and governance, but our focus ought to be on ministry, discipleship, outreach, justice, fellowship, and prayer.

In his book *I Refuse to Lead a Dying Church*, Paul Nixon writes, "My premise is this: that God intends every servant of the Resurrected Christ to be a servant of life. God has called all leaders, lay and clergy together, to lead healthy growing spiritual movements."[1] One of the churches I consulted in Connecticut had four leadership positions for every member of the church actively involved with the congregation. Through my consultation, I offered them a clear pathway for simplifying their system. This church system was screaming for change. However, they were still resistant to it. They lived in the basement of communication and had little hope of moving out. They had grown so accustomed to this chaotic system that reconfiguring it was too big a change. They preferred staying in the mess that they were in because this is what they had grown accustomed to. This church was clearly on a pathway toward death. The sad thing is that many church people would rather see their church die than change.

With regard to programs and ministries, original ideas are often generated by one person, but the plans are best implemented by a group. When church people work together in productive ways, they begin to resonate with the statement "two heads are better than one." When a leader's good ideas are lifted up before others they are often improved upon by the input offered by others. Task forces like these are at their best when trust-filled communication patterns are established. In general, churches have too many meetings, but there is something truly enjoyable about a meeting where good ideas are able to be expressed and applied. I find that working with others often enhances the work we do as pastors. Compromise is sometimes needed when you allow group interaction, but generally speaking this kind of interaction can lead into the creativity and community

1. Nixon, *Dying Church*, 3.

that we are seeking. Programs often feel more complete when plans are put into place by a group rather than an individual. Actually, it is not only two heads, but sometimes three, four, or five that are better. Small groups of people can offer the kind of programing and planning that needs extra attention or more precise action.

Flexibility

In his book *The Five Dysfunctions of a Team*, Patrick Lencioni suggests that the first two dysfunctions of a team are related to not enough trust in the system and too much fear of conflict.[2] Triangulation often erodes the trust levels that you establish within staff teams and leadership bodies. Any particular triangle may not seem overly destructive, but as these triangles accumulate and overlap with each other, major dysfunction can develop. In team settings and leadership bodies, we must be able to confront each other and discuss issues on a passionate level. We must be able to talk honestly with each other without the fear of breaking relationships. Most churches demand a certain level of spiritual and emotional maturity for their staff and leaders. If this is the case, direct communication will help your church to develop the kind of trust that will have a major impact.

Every staff relationship I have had has shaped and reshaped my approach to ministry. I have had the privilege of working with three youth ministers and two associate pastors. In all of these relationships, we have had to navigate the nonsense together. Compromise is one of the communication resources that we have had to rely on. However, in each case cooperation and collaboration have been the communication patterns we have preferred. These leaders have had the primary responsibility of the high school and middle school youth ministries. My relationship with each staff person has been unique because each one of them is a different person and because we have worked together during different phases and stages of the church's life. In each of these relationships, we have found that an occasional compromise can help us move through a difficult situation. This kind of flexibility has allowed us to reveal that we want to function as a team. Nevertheless, we have all found that too much compromise in staff relationships can be a particular problem. Improving communication patterns with your staff can help set the tone for board leaders and the congregation as a whole.

2. Lencioni, *Five Dysfunctions*, 188.

One example of a need for compromise arose during a conflict with one of my youth ministers in Connecticut. One of the unique things about youth ministry in this location was that the best time to work with students was on Sunday mornings. We were in a small town, and the students were beyond busy. I know high school students everywhere have a lot of activities, but in a small town school this is amplified. Students who were athletic often played a sport every season, and sometimes they were also in the school play or the school choir. Students who were talented in music or theater also filled in the gaps on the athletic fields. Most of the kids stayed extra busy at school, and what this meant was that Sunday mornings were the best time for students to devote to youth ministries. This led our youth pastor to propose running our primary high school youth ministry program during worship on Sunday mornings. He presented a very clear and well thought out proposal. He wanted to run a youth ministry program called "Wake-Up Call" during worship downstairs in the high school Sunday school room.

I liked the "Wake-Up Call" idea, but I did not agree with the philosophical approach. This youth minister came from a large church where separating the high school students from the adults was a common practice. This was not our practice, and I did not like this idea. This not only separated the students from worship, but it also meant that youth pastor would not be a part of leading worship. The problem is that he felt as strongly as I did about all of this. I remember having heated discussions about these issues in my office. I actually did not mind having this kind of argument with him. I liked his passion and was impressed by his creativity. I just did not like the idea of separating high school youth ministry completely from worship, yet I came to realize there might be room for a compromise. Before we had a chance to compromise, however, he spoke to one of the parents about the conflict. This church member emailed me the next day with her opinions on the subject. I had been "triangled" by this youth pastor, and I did not like how it felt. The situation immediately became more complicated. The problem with triangulation is that it limits your ability to develop trust and honesty in your relationships.

I confronted this youth minister and talked about it with him. I informed him that a pattern of indirect communication would lead to deeper issues. His response was interesting because he had served in a youth ministry internship at his home church before he took our position. He said that this church had very clear rules about this kind of communication.

He said that he did not think it would be as big a deal in a smaller church. Through this experience, he learned that it was. This indirect communication compromised my relationship with the woman who got caught in the middle. The conflict still led into an appropriate compromise. The students met during a time that overlapped with worship. The students and youth minister came upstairs for the sermon, the closing song, and communion. This also allowed the youth minister to participate in preaching and certain aspects of worship leading. "Wake-Up Call" ended up being a successful program, and it has changed in shape and form a few times since it was established. Please note that in this situation the confusion developed when one person took the issue outside of the relationship.

Sacred Cows

Sacred cows are cherished traditions that seem immovable and unchangeable within our congregations. One pastor I have been working with told me about a struggle that developed between her and her music director. There was a cherished tradition in her church, which her music director did not care for. This was a Scandinavian Christmas tradition called the Sankta Lucia pageant in their Christmas church traditions. This pageant was a small part of their church's annual Christmas program. The Sankta Lucia story had its roots in Italy, but it was fully embraced by Scandinavian people. This is one way churches with Scandanavian heritage in the United States have celebrated their heritage. The reason this part of the program was frustrating to the music director was that the larger program had a theme and this part of the program did not always fit in with the theme. The Sankta Lucia pageant felt like a sacred cow to the music director. The new senior pastor picked up on this. She immediately started joking in staff meetings about how they needed to figure out a way to get rid of it. She was using humor to keep the staff from taking this issue and themselves too seriously. They had a lot of laughs about this in their meetings. However, the senior pastor had no immediate plans to touch this sacred cow at this early stage in her ministry.

The new senior pastor was treating this issue lightheartedly and working under the assumption that what was said in staff meetings stayed in staff meetings. However, not everyone on the staff got this memo. The new senior pastor realized this on the night of her first Christmas program. The music director put together a tremendous program around the theme "peace on earth." The musicians all sounded great and the children's choir presented several songs including the Sankta Lucia pageant. After the program, however, several members of the choir frantically wanted to talk to the senior pastor about how she felt about the Sankta Lucia pageant. She was surprised that this was their entire focus. She explained that the entire program was wonderful. They said, "Yeah, but you're not going to get rid of Lucia are you?" It was then that she realized that she had been triangled.

The next day the senior pastor spoke with the music director. The music director confessed that she had told a few people that the senior pastor wanted to get rid of "Sankta Lucia." The music director got excited about the thought that the senior pastor was willing to consider a change. She jumped on this and tried to put the issue on the table without asking permission from the senior pastor. She was trying to speed up the process. However, what the triangle did instead was helped to "cement the sacred cow." The pageant was not a be-all-end-all program issue for this senior pastor. It was actually a much loved tradition in this church, and it was one of the few ways that church continued to celebrate its heritage. The senior pastor was far less concerned with this programmatic issue than she was with the way this information was shared outside of their staff meetings. They all learned a valuable lesson that day about managing information. They learned that what gets said in a staff meeting stays in a staff meeting unless the staff agrees to share the information with others. Triangulation can force a compromise in some situation, but rarely cultivates a culture of cooperation or collaboration.

Control

Personality types can have an impact on the unique ways we work together. One new pastor I was working with was striving for improvement in his relationship with their music director. The music director was at this church for a few years before he started. When he first met the music director, the director intentionally shared her Myers-Briggs personality type with him. The Myers-Briggs Type Inventory or the MBTI is a personality inventory that classifies your personality type. In a book called *Type Talk* the authors write, "The idea behind the MBTI was that it could be used to establish individual preferences and then to promote a more constructive use of the differences between people."[3] The music director clearly wanted her senior

3. Kroeger and Thuesen, *Type Talk*, 11.

pastor to know something about her unique personality. This new pastor had some experience with Myers-Briggs and knew what his own type was. He also did some research to see how their two personality types tended to interact with each other. What he discovered was that these two personality types have a hard time working together because both personality types like to be in charge. He did not overreact to this information. Instead he saw this as a challenge. He knew this would mean he would have to work extra hard at their relationship. He figured this would be a good learning experience, and it was.

The senior pastor worked very hard on being as cooperative as he could be, and they eventually had great success. The music director was very a talented young musician, and there was a clear upside to what she brought to the church. The one problem they had early on was that they tended to use compromise as a primary means for resolving conflict. They compromised on issues like music selection, scheduling issues, special service times, the order of worship, and the role of musicians in each service. The place they tended to bump heads the most was in worship planning, and after a while, the compromises began to pile up. This did not make either of them happy. So, they strove to collaborate more intentionally and eventually they found ways to improve their communication and decision-making. Their relationship became more collaborative and their work became more creative.

One example of this had to do with their junior choir. Their junior choir was a group consisting of students from first grade to sixth grade. The music director felt like it should begin in second grade so that all the students in the choir could read. Since there were no grades in between first grade and second grade, there was no room to compromise. Instead of meeting in the middle they strove to find a third way. They started a "cherub" choir for pre-K through the first grade. This allowed the junior choir to start in second grade. The more this pastor and music director cooperated and collaborated, the better their relationship became. It is interesting that their mutual desire to be "the one in charge" forced them to collaborate with each other. Too much compromise did not feel right to either of them, and this forced them into a new pattern of communication.

Control Issues

One Sunday morning on my way to church, I stopped at a convenience store for a coffee. After filling my cup, I moved to the counter and waited in line. While I was waiting a plexiglass case filled with cigarette lighters caught my attention. Some had pictures of Daffy Duck, Road Runner, and Bugs Bunny on them. My favorite design, however, was a black lighter with the words "I have issues" imprinted on it. This statement made me laugh. I am not a smoker, but I had an image of someone smoking two packs a day being vulnerable enough to say, "I have issues." I actually made a T-shirt for myself with these words on the front. Since then, I have not only found myself saying,"I have issues," but also that "we all have control issues" as well.

The story about Jesus washing the feet of his disciples reveals how control issues and our personality types can relate to the conflicts we experience. In John 13:5–15 it says,

> Then he poured water into a basin and began to wash the disciples' feet and to wipe them with the towel that was tied around him. He came to Simon Peter, who said to him, "Lord, are you going to wash my feet?" Jesus answered, "You do not know now what I am doing, but later you will understand." Peter said to him, "You will never wash my feet." Jesus answered, "Unless I wash you, you have no share with me." Simon Peter said to him, "Lord, not my feet only but also my hands and my head!" Jesus said to him, "One who has bathed does not need to wash, except for the feet, but is entirely clean. And you are clean, though not all of you." For he knew who was to betray him; for this reason he said, "Not all of you are clean." After he had washed their feet, had put on his robe, and had returned to the table, he said to them, "Do you know what I have done to you? You call me Teacher and Lord—and you are right, for that is what I am. So if I, your Lord and Teacher, have washed your feet, you also ought to wash one another's feet. For I have set you an example, that you also should do as I have done to you.

When Jesus washed the feet of his disciples Peter revealed that he had some control issues. Peter clearly wanted to be in control of this situation, but Jesus did not let him have the reins. There are times in all of our relationships with God when we need to surrender control and let go of the reins. Compromise is one way we are able to let go of control, but it is not always the most productive way. In this situation with Peter, Jesus is clearly teaching him about servant leadership, where we place the interests of others before our own.

Confrontation

Confrontation is a form of direct communication. Confrontation takes place when one person speaks to another person about a sensitive issue in a relationship. Most people see confrontation as a negative behavior. They see confrontation as a source of conflict. People think that if we avoid confrontation, we will avoid conflict. The truth is that confrontation enables us to address issues that rest beneath the surface in our relationships in the long run. When these issues go unaddressed then they can end up hurting our relationships. These issues erupt into conflict if they are not addressed appropriately. Confrontation is an appropriate and effective way to deal with such issues. Confrontation is a very direct form of communication. This kind of communication can at times lead us beyond compromise, to cooperation or collaboration. This is why in Ephesians 4:14–15 it says,

> We must no longer be children, tossed to and fro and blown about by every wind of doctrine, by people's trickery, by their craftiness in deceitful scheming. But speaking the truth in love, we must grow up in every way into him who is the head, into Christ.

Here the Apostle Paul makes it clear that we need to speak "the truth in love." He suggests that if confrontation is done in a spirit of love, it will be productive. In his book *Caring Enough to Confront: How to Understand and Express Your Deepest Feelings Toward Others*, David Augsburger writes about how trust is "the basic floor" of all relationships. He writes,

> Confrontation without a floor of trust is useless. Confrontation with a solid foundation of trust builds rapport, opens understanding, earns respect and will be heard.[4]

Confrontation does not create the issues themselves. It brings them to the surface. If issues need to be addressed, then it makes sense to talk about them. It makes sense to "speak the truth in love." The alternative is to wait around for the proverbial pot to boil over. Confrontation can help churches to avoid unnecessary emotional explosions that can arise out of unidentified and unresolved issues.

4. Augsburger, *Caring Enough to Confront*, 79.

This is why in Matthew 18:15 Jesus says, "If another member of the church sins against you, go and point out the fault when the two of you are alone." This verse suggests there is an appropriate way to confront issues that regularly arise within our relationships. It requires a reasonable pace and a regular dose of direct communication. Not every issue requires confrontation, nor do we need to confront people aggressively about everything that comes up. If the people we are confronting know they are loved, then it should be easier. If a person does not know that he or she is loved, then confrontation is more difficult. Sadly some people habitually sweep things under the rug in their lives. They do this to avoid conflict in general. By avoiding conflict they actually end up avoiding the people themselves. These people may not initially enjoy confrontations, but they will appreciate positive results from these conversations in the long run.

Sometimes conversations shake things up a little bit in our relationships. Only people who care about a relationship will have the will to confront someone to improve the relationship. Confrontation forces people to talk directly to others. It keeps you from talking about others. It encourages you to enter into open and honest conversations with them. This kind of direct communication minimizes the number of triangles generated within your congregation. It forces pastors and church leaders out of the pattern of avoiding the people with whom they have disagreements. Church leaders are typically surprised by how good this can feel. Confrontation does not cause conflict—it helps us to address it.

Avoiding conflict by refusing to confront issues does not make you a peacemaker. When Jesus said "Blessed are the peacemakers," he was not honoring those who avoid conflict. There is a big difference between making peace and avoiding conflict, just as there is a big difference from meeting someone in the middle and being in the middle of someone else's conflict. Continuing his conversation about confrontation in Matthew 18:15–16, Jesus says, "If the member listens to you, you have regained that one. But if you are not listened to, take one or two others along with you, so that every word may be confirmed by the evidence of two or three witnesses." The reason Jesus encourages us to work things out directly with those who sin against us is because this opens up communication. He encourages us to begin with one-on-one conversations. Then he suggests going with two or three witnesses, if the issues are not resolved in this first meeting. Avoiding conflict can actually create bigger issues and deeper levels of conflict. Addressing conflict directly and regularly helps churches to acknowledge that things within the church are not as they should be. This is why peacemakers have to be people who communicate at a high level. These people encourage others to talk about the real issues plaguing relationships. They also help their congregations to embrace communication patterns that aid them to address issues that others may be tempted to ignore.

Several years ago, a disagreement emerged in my congregation. Some people in the church wanted to embark on a building project. The building was over forty years old and had several identified issues. Plans were developed to expand our building and to renovate certain parts of our building. When the plans were presented to the congregation, there was not enough support to move forward. Some people were clearly concerned about the amount of money this project would cost. Other people were simply concerned about the plan itself. They were not sure that we were getting the best return possible on the investment that would be required. So, we tabled the discussion at the end of that year. When the newly elected Executive Board began meeting in the next year, we asked a different question. We took the total planned cost of the project and considered the best way we could use that kind of money to improve our facilities. We moved our focus off the minor expansion we were considering and onto a thorough renovation of our facilities. We rearranged the walls of our classrooms to eliminate the need for expansion and focused on much needed renovation. This was a compromise that eventually led into the fruitful cooperation of our leaders and participation of our church members.

The vice chairperson of our church gave shape to this renovation project and capital campaign. She asked a wide range of people from the church to be on several small committees that focused on the specific need for improvements in each part of our church building. She simply asked these committees to generate ideas and come up with estimated budgets for the work necessary to complete these renovations. There was a kitchen committee, a sanctuary committee, a back entrance committee, and a lounge committee. These committees met long before the congregation was asked to consider the comprehensive renovation plan. These four committees did not meet all together until just before a proposal would be made to the congregation about the plans in general. The amazing thing about this was that all these plans were tied together into one rather cohesive proposal at this meeting. The people on these committees also began to buy into the overall proposal before it was delivered to the congregation. People not only supported this plan with their vote, but also with financial support.

This creative use of committees helped us to establish the vision and the momentum for this church-wide project. It allowed a wide range of people to be involved with several parts of one big project, and it encouraged buy-in from a lot of our church members. There was some compromise, but this led to a lot of cooperation and collaboration. When we compromise, all parties feel like they have lost something. Cooperation and collaboration are much better places to be when working together. More often than not, cooperation and collaboration are attainable goals. Sometimes compromise helps people to maintain chemistry in working relationships. All of these levels of communication are a necessary part of a team environment. However, the goal for all churches is to hover in the higher elevations.

BEST PRACTICE #2

Church Governance

With regard to church governance, my strong recommendation is that congregations have one governing body and several ministry teams. My general experience is that one governing body is enough for any pastor to interact with, and that two governing bodies will inevitably result in triangulation, confusion, and chaos. In Attleboro, the Executive Board focuses on governance, and the other groups focus on ministry. Dan Hotchkiss wrote a great book, *Governance and Ministry*, which helps churches to understand the difference between these two realities. In this book, he writes,

> Some congregations have two, or even three, top boards, all responsible directly to the congregation. Sometimes the division reflects an old-fashioned mom-and-pop dualism: the trustees (Dad) control the money, while a program board (Mom) does all the work. Sometimes one board is said to be responsible for the "business" aspects of the congregation, while the other takes charge of the "spiritual" part. Have I made it clear yet that I don't like this way of splitting up the universe.[5]

Hotchkiss and I strongly agree on this matter. Such a dualism creates a culture of triangulation between the primary leadership groups of a congregation. It puts the senior pastor in a perpetual pattern of triangulation with these groups. I often say that when churches are set up for disaster, we

5. Hotchkiss, *Governance*, 53.

should not be surprised when disaster strikes. Hotchkiss goes on to say, "A congregation can create as many boards as it wants, though legally the state will recognize only one of them as 'the board.'"[6] This does not mean that the courts should dictate how we do church, but I do believe that the reason a court will only recognize one group as "the board" is because it would be far too confusing otherwise. This is true for regional and denominational leaders as well. If I were a denominational leader working with churches, I would recognize only one group as "the board."

One first-call pastor I have been working with illustrated her emotional response to this kind of dualism by saying that she felt like the daughter of divorced parents trying to mediate between their disagreements. She gave me the example of a memorial bench. Someone donated a memorial bench to the church in memory of a loved one who died tragically at a young age. The primary concern of the trustees was to make sure that the people donating the bench would understand that the church has a policy about not having plaques on memorial donations. The Deacons saw this issue as secondary to the way this bench would minister to the family, even if it had a plaque. The pastor felt caught in the middle of these two groups and their competing concerns. The reason this got so confusing and chaotic was that the pastor was caught in the middle of a triangle between herself and the two distinct governing bodies. In my mind, this is no way to run a business, let alone a church. If she was reporting to one governing body in the church, then they would be concerned about finding a balance between this policy and the ministry taking place.

This "mom-and-pop dualism" is a consistent problem in many of the churches I have consulted. Many of these congregations have had a Deacon Board and a Trustee Board that share the responsibility of church governance. In these cases, the Deacon Board is supposed to pay attention to the spiritual matters whereas the Trustee Board is supposed to pay attention to the financial and facility matters. On paper this seems rather clean and clear. One group pays attention to the cold hard facts, and the other group tends to the programs and the people. The sad thing is that pastors and parishioners often get triangled between these two groups. This division of labor forces churches into the basement of communication. This dualism not only leads them into the communication basement, but it tends to keep them there. The pastors in these churches all end up feeling like

6. Ibid., 53.

the children of divorced parents. They lack vision and their ministries feel frozen in place.

In my first book, *Challenging the Church Monster,* I recommend a single-board system for small churches. I wrote about how we eliminated all other boards at Salem Covenant Church. This type of single-board system works well for a church of around 100 people. I am currently serving a church of around 300 people, and having several ministry teams works very well in this environment. In this current church system, however, we have an Executive Board that focuses on church governance. The Deacon Board, Trustee Board, Board of Christian Education, and Mission and Outreach Board all have specific responsibilities. Each one of these boards focuses on their particular areas of ministry. They focus on ministries and activities of the church, not on church governance. The Executive Board focuses on things like budgets, staff, annual meetings, elections, policies, major decisions, capital improvements, and building renovations. The big decisions and overall supervision of the ministries lies in the hands of the Executive Board. Ministry and programs are the work of the other ministry teams.

ZONE II: THE MAIN FLOORS

Level two churches are churches that hover between cooperation and collaboration. They work hard at communication and ministry. These churches typically have a lot on their agenda, and they tend to be at their best when they have a lot going on. Level two churches do experience conflict and compromise, but they get frustrated if either conflict or compromise gets in the way of ministry. Some of these churches need to learn how to work smarter, not harder, and they sometimes forget to allow room for the Holy Spirt. Level two churches hover around "the main floors." The main floors in most buildings are the places where the work gets done. The main floors of a hospital are the places where patients are served directly by doctors and nurses. The main floors in office buildings are the places you will find cubicles, small offices, and the meeting rooms where much work is accomplished. The main floors are not the basement where you will find the mail room, the furnace room, or the garbage shoots. It is also not the set of floors where you find executive offices and large meeting suites. This is where the mission of the organization is fulfilled, not supported or overseen. The main floors tend to be filled with people who take care of the nitty-gritty, day-to-day implementation of an organization. They are filled with people who work hard and pay attention to the details of daily operations. Cooperation and collaboration take a lot of hard work, and the more we employ these patterns of communication in our churches, the more we will be able to stay out of the basement and function at this higher level. This type of communication also allows us to discover pathways toward the higher elevations of creativity and community.

chapter 3

Cooperation

Cooperation is what happens when individuals and groups share responsibility in a coordinated fashion. It is working together in an organized and productive way. Cooperation helps organizations to function at a high level. It has to do with the systems we develop that allow this to happen. One strength of cooperation is that it can be done without spending the kind of time that is required for collaboration. Collaboration is working on one thing together. Cooperation is working separately on two or more things that come together in one direction. Cooperation is working side by side in one accord or for one purpose. Even though collaboration can produce high-quality results, it can be time consuming, and it may not always be necessary. Many projects actually require both cooperation and collaboration. The key to effectively managing projects or responsibilities is related to discerning when collaboration is needed and where cooperation can save time. Finding the right balance between cooperation and collaboration has to do with working independently and interactively. Cooperation is typically the most appropriate path when a ministry team has a limited amount of time and energy to get everything done.

Trust

Mark Novak is the Executive Minister of the Ordered Ministry within our denomination. He is currently the top-level leader in our church who deals with credentialed clergy and the issues we face. I recently heard him speak about developing "high-trust culture" in our churches. He clearly indicated that dysfunctional church staff relationships were among his greatest concerns as a denominational leader. I am convinced that ministry teams ultimately need to figure out how to share authority and responsibility effectively. Clarifying roles helps individuals to understand their place within a congregational system. Clarifying roles also helps staff teams to discern when collaboration is necessary and when cooperation is more appropriate. One of the things that Mark said in his presentation was that when we don't have trust, we tend to want control.[1] Control issues are at the heart of perpetual staff conflict situations. Learning how to share authority and responsibility through cooperation and collaboration improves communication and strengthens staff teams, and also relationships between pastors and lay leaders. Trust is the foundation upon which faithful and fruitful ministry is conducted.

When my church in Connecticut called its first youth minister, we got a young man who happened to be six feet, eight inches tall with a thick head of blond hair. This was his first position right out of college. On his candidating weekend while he was interacting with church members in the entrance area of our church, I was standing there and talking with an eighth-grade student. She looked at this tall young man and said to me, "Pastor Bixby, you're going to have to share your authority with him." I looked back at her and said, "You are right." She nodded, as if to say that she was simply making an observation. It was, however, one of the most profound things I had ever heard someone say about leadership. I have seen plenty of staff teams fail to function or even fall apart because of their failure to share authority in appropriate ways.

Leaders who trust each other enough to share authority and responsibility can have a dramatic impact on any congregation. Senior pastors get into trouble when they share responsibility without authority. This often happens because senior pastors feel threatened by the abilities of those working for them. Fear keeps them from sharing enough authority with the responsibility. The fear is that if a staff person shines, then the glow around their personal ministry might diminish. The truth is that when an effective staff person functions at a high level, this typically makes the senior pastor look good, not bad. Someone else functioning at a high level should not be seen as a threat by the senior pastor, but a boost to your ministries. The glory is God's, not ours. Problems arise, however, when egos get in the way and when power struggles develop. When this happens leaders stop

1. This presentation was made by Mark Novak at the East Coast Conference 2015 Annual Meeting of the Evangelical Covenant Church, Salem Covenant Church in Worcester, Massachusetts.

believing that God can bring out the best in all of us. We all need trust-filled relationships with God and each other that allow space for the mystery of Christ to emerge from within our ministries.

Sabbaticals are great opportunities for pastors to experience rest from ministry and renewal for ministry. I have noticed, however, that staff teams tend to do a good job planning for sabbaticals before they happen, but they rarely put enough time into planning for the return of the senior pastor. On more than one occasion I have observed staff teams struggle with sharing authority when a senior pastor returns from a sabbatical. Some senior pastors develop ego-related issues with staff members who manage things well while they are away. These senior pastors freely share the responsibility and authority of their position when they go on sabbatical because this allows them to do so. However, when they return things feel different. In these situations it would be wise for staff teams to plan on this return and to creatively share authority in new ways as the staff team rediscovers its equilibrium. It is important to realize that ministry is not a competition. All staff members have strengths and all staff teams need to figure out how to best take advantage of each other's differences. None of us are perfect and all of us need to discover how God wants us to work together. I recently heard from a senior pastor who found hospital visitation burdensome and did not see it as one of his strengths. His associate pastor enjoyed doing the hospital visitation while he was on sabbatical. The senior pastor began sharing these responsibilities more fluidly with her upon his return from sabbatical. This new way of sharing ministry responsibilities made a big difference in their church. Sabbatical transition periods clearly provide staff teams with great opportunities for new beginnings in terms of redefining roles and responsibilities.

Authority

Discerning how to divide responsibility and authority with your staff team can be challenging. Sometimes churches divide things programmatically, or by age groups, or by designated areas of responsibility. Some large churches have executive pastors that focus on administration, discipleship pastors that focus on spiritual formation, visitation pastors that focus on pastoral care, youth pastors that focus on middle school and high school youth ministries, and/or children's pastors that focus on programs like Sunday school and Vacation Bible School. However, most churches only have one or two full-time pastors. And when there are two, the associate pastor typically focuses on particular areas of responsibility, and yet responsibilities often overlap, and ministry opportunities are sometimes shared by staff and church leaders. Sometimes problems arise when these areas of responsibility are too clearly defined or not clearly defined enough. When positions are too clearly defined there is not enough flexibility, and when they are not defined enough they lack structure. Positions that are too clearly defined can keep your staff isolated from each other and alienated from certain portions of the congregation. In an ideal situation there will be room for both cooperation and collaboration in all of our working relationships. This kind of interaction with each other often leads to the kind of creativity and community for which all churches long.

The most common staff position in churches is in the area of music ministry. A lot of small churches have one pastor and a part-time music director. In Connecticut, we had a part-time music director named Susan. She is still there and has been the choir director at Salem Covenant Church for more than two decades. She is a great leader and very gifted musician. She played piano at Carnegie Hall in New York City on several occasions. I often felt blessed to have someone with her credentials in this part-time position. One of the reasons she was content with a part-time position was because she was raising two young twin boys while we served together. Her boys were the same age as my oldest daughter. The age of our kids and the part-time nature of this position forced us to be more cooperative than collaborative. We simply divided the planning responsibilities. I picked the congregational hymns and songs and she picked the choral and special music. We did not spend a lot of time working together. In all honesty, I preferred that she spend her collaborative hours with the other musicians rather than me. We had a great choir and praise team and these musicians enjoyed the creative and collaborative work they did with Susan. I picked the hymns and songs because of their connection with the sermon and the service. We occasionally offered suggestions and encouragement to each other, but we generally maintained this division of labor throughout our fifteen years working together.

This cooperative model worked well for Susan and me. We were often surprised by the way things fit together in worship on Sunday mornings. This does not mean that collaboration would have been a bad path for us. It is just to say that we were able to manage things effectively through cooperation. It was the best way to manage our responsibilities at the time, and it kept us both involved with worship planning. The services were ours, not hers or mine. I am now in a larger church with a full-time director of music ministries, and we work more collaboratively with each other. We select the congregational hymns and songs in our services collaboratively, and we talk specifically about how things will work together in each service. In both situations, the key ingredient to success is a positive, trust-filled relationship. In both churches I have served, I have learned to stay out of the middle of the selection of choir and special music. I leave this up to the musicians. This helps us to avoid triangulation, and it forces the musicians and their director to work creatively together. This also encourages the musicians to take responsibility for the direction of their music ministries. This is one way I have been able to share both authority and responsibility with my music directors and the church musicians.

Responsibility

Spiritual formation is one arena that can effectively employ both cooperation and collaboration. Team teaching is one way that authority and responsibility can be shared by pastors and staff. One example of cooperation in my current church is related to our confirmation and discipleship program. This is a two-year program for seventh- and eighth-grade students in our church. Every Thursday in Attleboro, we meet with over a dozen seventh- and eighth-grade students who come each week to spend an hour with their two pastors. We sit in a large circle and focus on the foundations of the Christian faith. Teaching this class on a weekly basis is a significant commitment for both pastors in our church. When I arrived in Attleboro, I discovered that my associate pastor was accustomed to sharing the teaching of this class with my predecessor. They both participated in the teaching of each class session. This required a significant amount of collaboration before each session, and the balance of authority and responsibility was always a work in progress.

In my mind, the time requirement for this type of collaboration seemed ominous, and the task of dividing the responsibilities seemed tedious, especially in the first few months of my ministry. So I suggested that we alternate the teaching role each week. I would teach one week and he would teach the next. He agreed and we both participate in each class session as small group discussion leaders, but only one of us is in charge of preparing the lesson each week, including the discussion questions we both use. Cooperation is clearly more efficient than collaboration, but in this case, we also think it was more effective. This way of team teaching not only saved us time, but it also gave the students the opportunity to hear two different voices and perspectives in the teaching. It was an easy way to share both responsibility and authority. Leading small discussion groups each week includes both pastors in the important task of relationship building, but this cooperative approach minimizes the amount of time and energy we have to put into preparation for each class session.

Another blessing that developed as a result of this cooperation was additional form of cooperation. One Thursday I noticed that my associate pastor was setting up the chairs in the classroom we were using. The furniture in the room we were using for this class typically needed to be rearranged each week. This was not terribly time consuming, but it was always a bit of a burden. When I noticed that my associate pastor was setting up the room for me when I was teaching, I started reciprocating. After a while, we agreed this was also a good way for us to share responsibilities even further. So, we developed a pattern of setting up the room for the class sessions we were not scheduled to teach. In this case, one form of cooperation led into another, and this innovation clearly helped us to feel supported by each other.

With regard to these discipleship responsibilities I actually enjoy preparing the lesson when I am teaching, and I feel good about having to do a little physical labor on the weeks I am not. I know this is not rocket science, but finding ways to make things function in the church is always a good thing. My associate pastor and I were not averse to talking with one another or collaborating on our lessons, but we were both grateful for a system that helped us to share ministry more efficiently. This level of cooperation also makes room for us to collaborate on other things that need extra attention. As leaders we need to pay attention to the small things if we want the big things to take place. Hovering between cooperation and collaboration is a great place to be. Discerning between cooperation and collaboration is always a matter of stewardship. It has to do with wisely using the time, energy, and talents of those involved with a staff team and a church community. Striving to figure out the best balance between cooperation and collaboration is a critical matter for any team striving to share authority and responsibility in effective ways.

Complaining

Complaining is another challenging roadblock to clear communication. One biblical example of complaining comes from the story of Mary and Martha. This story also reveals how Jesus dealt with complainers. The story is found in Luke 10:38–42. It says,

> Now as they went on their way, Jesus entered a certain village, where a woman named Martha welcomed him into her home. She had a sister named Mary, who sat at the Lord's feet and listened to what he was saying. But Martha was distracted by her many tasks; so she came to him and asked, "Lord, do you not care that my sister has left me to do all the work by myself? Tell her then to help me." But the Lord answered her, "Martha, Martha, you are worried and distracted by many things; there is need of only one thing. Mary has chosen the better part, which will not be taken away from her."

Martha was essentially complaining to Jesus about Mary's behavior. Here you can clearly see how Martha invited Jesus into the middle of the relationship issue she had with Mary. Jesus responded by essentially saying he was not going to get into the middle of it. However, he did not mind using this situation to reveal something about the difference between what the world values and what God values.

Through this story Jesus clearly revealed his appreciation for the quieter virtues of contemplation, discernment, and listening. Jesus was in no way casting judgment on hospitality. As a matter of fact, hospitality was something he encouraged and appreciated in many other portions of Scripture. Jesus once said that he "came to serve, not to be served" (Matt 20:28). With regard to Mary and Martha Jesus simply used this triangle as a teachable moment. If he had sided with Martha in this situation, he would have been directly in the middle. On the other hand, by siding with Mary he was forcing Martha to deal with their differences more directly at a better time. Martha was the one trying to pull Jesus into middle, and I am convinced that Jesus resisted triangulation for a reason. Jesus was confronting Martha's complaining and triangulation. He simply did not want to be used as a tool for leverage with regard to Martha's relationship issues with Mary. He clearly did not want Martha to drag him into this triangle with her complaining.

The relationship issues between Mary and Martha was something they would have to figure out on their own. Jesus was not going to do this for them. Jesus knew they needed to talk directly about it when he was not in the room. Jesus would have made this conflict more complicated by getting in the middle of it. Sometimes church members can draw attention to themselves through the same kind of public complaining that Martha was doing. We often call this "drama" in our contemporary relationships. When you are working in a group, there are always opportunities to complain about others, but Jesus reveals that it is always better to confront directly than it is to complain indirectly. When people complain enough in the church, they begin to feel entitled to it, and church leaders want to find ways to respond to every complaint. If we are unable to respond to the complainer, we often freeze up with regard to our relationships and responsibilities. Overly reactive leadership is time consuming and distracting. It can also become discouraging. Churches never satisfy everyone's needs nor should they be expected to. This type of reactive leadership is one of the reasons why so many churches are inclined toward hovering in the basement between conflict and compromise.

I am not only a pastor. I am also a parent. When my children complain about work they are asked to do around the house, I tell them to stop complaining. Or, if they are grumbling about their homework, I encourage them to get it done. I also coach my daughter's soccer team. Players often complain about running too much. When they do this, I tell them to stop complaining, or they will have to run another lap. In the church we at times encourage complaining more than we discourage it. Many churches even make themselves available for special times to hear complaints. Church leaders recognize that there are issues in our churches, and we extend ample opportunity for people to share their concerns. The problem is that complaining rarely leads people to bear responsibility. Complainers typically are looking for other people to solve the problems. This is why I think structured meetings that are focused on seeking solutions are far more productive than open forums for leaders to hear complaints. We need to give church members more opportunities to solve problems, not complain about them.

In Galatians 6:2 it says, "Bear one another's burdens, and in this way you will fulfill the law of Christ." A few verses later it says, "All must carry their own loads" (Gal 6:5). This is saying that we need to have low expectations with regard to others helping us and high expectations with regard to the help we offer to others. The big choice here is between complaining about problems and solving them. This is how Christian community is developed. It is not established by us focusing on how other people have failed us. It is established when we take responsibility for ourselves and the needs of others within our communities. If we keep the expectations we have of others low and "carry our own load," then other people will occasionally surprise us with their help and support. And if we are all trying to "bear one another's burdens," then we may surprise each other more often than not. What this Scripture reveals is that church people need to stop focusing on whether or not their needs are being met and to start focusing on whether or not we are meeting the needs of others. This will help us to have high expectation for ourselves and reasonable expectations of others.

Promises

Pastors often find themselves in the middle of triangles with regard to other people's marriage problems. Imagine John enters a pastor's office one Sunday after worship and says that he wants to talk about Bill and Sally. Also imagine that you are the pastor and this is your office. You respond caringly and ask, "What is it?" He says that Bill and Sally are having marriage problems, and he wants to know if you will to go and talk with them about these problems. Many good-hearted pastors feel obligated to say "yes" in these situations, even if they are not comfortable with it. They say "yes" because they think this is what they are supposed to say. The reason they feel uncomfortable approaching Bill and Sally is because neither Bill nor Sally have acknowledged the problem to the pastor. This situation has the potential of putting the pastor, John, and the couple in a highly charged emotional triangle. One way for the pastor to avoid the triangle is to encourage John to talk with Bill and Sally and recommend that they come and make an appointment to talk with you, the pastor, about their marriage problems.

Suppose you, as the pastor, go to Bill and Sally and say, "I hear you have marriage problems." They are now going to want to know who the source was. This leaves the pastor in an awkward situation. Thus the best way to avoid a triangle is for John to recommend that Bill and Sally set up an appointment with the pastor. Asking John to encourage direct communication enables John to bear some of the responsibility. It also keeps you from making promises that you cannot keep. John clearly broke the confidence of his friend when, without permission, he shared this information with the pastor. One of the reasons he did this is because he does not feel equipped to deal with their marriage issues. So to be clear, John did not do anything wrong by sharing this information with his pastor. He was in over his head and he needed someone with which to talk.

Problems would develop, however, if the pastor were to make promises to John about how he could help. The outcome ultimately depends on what the pastor does with this information. The only other way for the pastor to avoid this triangle is to approach the couple about their marriage issues without sharing this particular information. If there are other visible signs of brokenness that allow this pastor to enter into a conversation, then he or she could begin this conversation without divulging the information that John shared. There is a big difference between the pastor saying "I have not seen you together in church lately. Is everything okay?" and "I heard that you are having marriage problems." One avoids a triangle. The other places you in the middle of one.

As pastors and church leaders, we are at times grateful when someone comes to us and is concerned about a marriage. We like it when someone trusts us to come and talk with us about significant relational matters, even when they are not theirs. We promise to help because we want to appear helpful. We promise to help in the hope that we will look significant to others. The problem is that these emotional triangles keep us from being effective. We must be aware of the difficulty of helping people who have not asked for our help directly. We can pay attention to these individuals and relationships, but we must acknowledge the challenge we face when trying to help people who have not asked for help. Attempts to do this often fall short. Triangles like these actually break trust more than they build trust. When this happens, the people in our churches often end up avoiding our help rather than seeking it. If we wait patiently for people to come and talk about their issues with us, then it will be based on trust, not manipulation. Each time we allow a triangle to get the best of us, we feel more depleted and helpless. This kind of triangulation can have a devastating long-term impact on our ministries. Triangulation has a cumulative negative impact.

Information

The Alban Institute once asked Karen McClintock and I to collaborate on a spiritual practices program called SLASH, which was cosponsored by the Center for Renewal. Karen co-wrote a book with Kibbie Simmons Ruth called *Healthy Disclosure: Solving Communication Quandaries in*

Congregations. In this book they coin the phrase "pass-through communication." They write, "Some congregations get in the habit of pass-through communication. To get a message to someone, you tell someone else."[2] They identify this type of communication as a subtle form of triangulation. They also encourage churches to discourage it. They suggest that, "Informal channels of pass-through communication lead to misunderstandings down the road. Like the children's telephone game, the content usually becomes distorted and often the necessary action delayed."[3] What I have discovered in this regard is that avoiding triangulation is a good practice no matter how large or small the issue is.

Avoiding "pass-through communication" helps to protect marriage relationships, and it improves communication within the church system. My wife and I started avoiding "pass-through communication" before we even had a name for it. We did this instinctively to protect our relationship. Since I entered the ministry, my wife Carolyn and I have agreed that we will always refuse to pass bits of information to one another. If someone speaks to my wife and says, "Would you tell your husband . . . ," she quickly responds, "No, you need to talk with him directly." I have also noticed that people rarely get upset when she makes these requests for direct communication. They simply say "Okay." They also stop making the requests after a while. After reading about "pass-through communication" I realized that no matter how big or small the issue is triangulation is still triangulation, and the more we avoid it the better our communication is and the stronger our relationships are. I now know why my wife and I made this agreement over twenty years ago, and it has helped us.

Some church people also assume they can pass information along from one staff person to another because they work together on a daily basis. Agreeing to pass information along may feel cooperative at the time, but it actually has a negative impact on cooperation. "Pass-through communication" creates little triangles. And these little triangles seem innocuous at first because they can be formed around mundane issues like calendaring and program details. Nevertheless, the miscommunication that can take place when the information does not get passed on can create major issues. Avoiding this kind of miscommunication should be a priority of your church. When staff members, spouses, and other church leaders avoid

2. Ruth and McClintock, *Healthy Disclosure*, 188.

3. Ibid, 189.

"pass-through communication," your communication patterns throughout the church system improve.

A first-call pastor once told me about an awkward situation in her church where she felt triangled. A member of her church asked her to bring a gift to the director of a small retreat center. This was a place where their congregation held an annual leadership retreat. This person painted a water color of a bench in the woods on the retreat center grounds. The church member really liked his painting. He had it framed and wanted to give it to the retreat center as a gift. This person knew that the pastor was visiting the retreat center soon and asked her to give this framed picture to the director. It was a nice gesture, and the pastor agreed to do this. However, once she agreed, she started to feel uncomfortable. The problem with accepting this responsibility was that she did not know if the director of the retreat center would want to hang this picture up. She was afraid the director would feel forced to do this because of who was delivering it. Suppose the director did not like the painting, but felt obligated to hang it up, because this person was not merely a delivery person, she was the pastor of a church that paid to use their facilities. This pastor did not like feeling like the delivery of this gift was forcing the director's hand. She also did not like feeling that the gift giver might be disappointed if the retreat center did not hang it up. She was completely in the middle of this situation, and the person who painted the picture did not have to bear any of the emotional responsibility.

This pastor realized that she should have encouraged the church member to share the gift directly himself. The gift would have meant more if it came directly from the person who was giving it. Thus, the pastor could have said to the giver, "It would mean more if it came directly from you." Refusing this responsibility would have put the emotional responsibility back on the shoulders of the gift giver, and it would have taken the pastor out of the middle. This pastor ended up feeling like she should have refused this role of being the delivery person, but at the end of the day she knew that this was not a huge issue. She learned a valuable lesson, however, about avoiding "pass-through communication" the next time it arises. None of these examples of "pass-through communication" are in and of themselves devastating. It is the accumulation of various triangles of all sizes that weakens relationships and causes conflict to escalate. Real systemic issues arise when habitual patterns of indirect communication are developed. Slowing down our responses and asking for time to consider requests is better than an impatient response. Quickly saying yes to every request made can get us into trouble. A more reflective approach to our responses can help us to be more productive. Leaving these issues unattended will eventually lead into significant issues. We should not underestimate the potential impact of the cumulative effect of these little triangles.

Administration

The way church offices function or fail to function reveals how paying attention to the small things can make a big difference in our churches. Carol has been a highly respected church secretary and office manager for over thirty years at our church. She is a natural at direct communication. One of her strengths is that she does not get into the middle of conflicts. She clearly refers people with concerns to the appropriate people. It would be difficult for a person to stay in a position like this for more than three years, let alone thirty, if they fail to avoid triangular relationships. Carol not only knows how to coordinate the efforts of our church leaders and staff, but she also has a tremendous amount of institutional knowledge. Carol knows when things need to get done, and she typically knows who is supposed to do them. Church secretaries who create triangles on a regular basis are not only a liability, but they typically burn out quickly. An office manager who can effectively avoid triangles is a huge asset to any congregation.

One very important tool for cooperation is a centralized calendar. When you have a variety of different groups and leaders trying to utilize one building with a limited amount of space, you need a central calendar for all meetings and activities to be posted. This helps you to avoid scheduling conflicts and unnecessary arguments. Our office manager may be a wise communicator, but she is not clairvoyant. She needs people to cooperate with her. Failing to write dates down on our church-wide calendar keeps meetings and events from being announced in our church newsletter and bulletins. Effective communication not only has to be direct and honest, but it also has to be clear and organized. When you are working with a staff team or a group of lay leaders, a lack of clarity in communication with each other can lead to unnecessary breakdowns in relationships. Clear communication patterns and systems will help churches to keep chaos to a minimum. This can also be done electronically. Even though I have been suggesting that we need to avoid triangulation not conflict, it does not make sense to consistently create unnecessary conflicts. Having a system like a centralized calendar is one example of a way you can do this.

Another example of a simple system like this is church office mailboxes. When I arrived in Attleboro, I noticed that there were no staff mailboxes in the church office. The only way to pass information to my music director or associate pastor was to place an envelope on his or her desk and hope they found it. One of the first purchases the church made after I arrived was a large wooden wall-mounted file system. It was put up in the office and is now used as staff mailboxes. We have a mailbox for all the pastors, the staff members, and the board chairs. This allows us to pass information directly and discretely to each other without a great deal of confusion. The staff and board chair mailboxes also help our administrative secretary to deliver the mail that comes into the office more easily. Cooperation and communication go hand in hand.

Staff meetings are also an important tool for navigating the nonsense in our churches. They help churches develop a team approach. We have staff meetings each week in Attleboro. The primary purpose of these meetings is to avoid confusion and coordinate our efforts. In these meetings, we strive to make sure we are all on the same page with regard to our calendars and programing. We begin each staff meeting by reflecting back on the previous week. We talk about good moments and God moments. This is a reflection on the significant things that happened in our lives and ministries during the past week. Sometimes we reflect on worship and programs. Other times we focus on people and relationships. We also talk about our families or major events in our lives. We strive to see where God is working, and we celebrate the things that are happening in our lives, with our families, or at our church. After this, one of us will pray over our meeting and typically give thanks for these God things and good things. After this we talk about our worship plans, calendaring for the week, month, and year. We talk about our hopes and about obvious ways we can coordinate our efforts and collaborate with each other. We talk about pastoral concerns and the visitors and newcomers we saw in the past week. I even notice that our music director shares in the visitation efforts as a result of these conversations and her compassion for others.

In some ways staff meetings do not always feel significant because they tend to be so straightforward. However, direct communication about the calendar and programmatic details can help us to avoid a lot of unnecessary conflict. Gil Rendle and Susan Beaumont write extensively about staff meetings in their book *When Moses Meets Aaron: Staffing and Supervision in Large Congregations*. They comment,

> Staff meetings are not gatherings in which everyone must participate in every conversation, be involved in all decisions, and reach unanimous agreement. Information sharing is not the same as group decision making. Collaboration and alignment of effort are not the same as approaching an issue or a question as a "work of the whole." Decisions belong to the persons or groups who have authority and accountability for making something happen. Staff meetings in which the team is built and information is shared are still good meetings—even if no decisions are made.[4]

Open communication about the programs and activities in the church that are functioning or not functioning is essential. There are times when independently keeping up with all the ministry-related details and people-related issues in the ministry of a church can become overwhelming for church leaders and their staff. Sharing this responsibility through staff meetings can help minimize anxiety and keep ministries moving forward without unnecessary interruptions.

Paying attention to ministry details can help us to discover the joy of cooperation and collaboration. One of my colleagues informed me that his church resolved a simple issue for their coffee hour during a staff meeting. This church used to ask individuals to make the coffee and to make the baked goods for their coffee hour. They noticed, however, that there were some people in the church who liked to bake and were not baking for their coffee hour. They discovered that this was because they did not feel comfortable making the coffee with the church coffee makers. They also noticed some people did not make coffee because they did not like to bake. When they separated these two sign-up sheets, they discovered more people were participating in the process of preparing for their coffee hour needs. It was a simple change that took place because they were willing to talk about what was working and what was not in a staff meeting.

Although coffee may seem insignificant to some people, it has a lot of significance for others. This may be why I chose this subject. Coffee was also the centerpiece of another learning experience for a local church. This church learned to periodically let things fall through the cracks helped with the coffee hour sign-up. This church was accustomed to having coffee set up in between services each Sunday. When the people arrived and the hot coffee was not on the counters the people were not happy. The person in charge of finding people to make the coffee reminded people about where

4. Rendle and Beaumont, *Moses Meets Aaron*, 196.

they could sign up. The amazing thing is that everyone who was disappointed that day survived, but more importantly the sign-up sheet was filled by the end of that Sunday morning. When these thirsty people did not get their coffee, the list quickly filled up. Problems arise if you have individual leaders who always come to the rescue.

What this church discovered is that the best leadership does not always jump in and fix a problem. Rescuers often get discouraged because of the amount of responsibility they take on. So, the theory is that the best leadership occasionally allows things to fall through the cracks. I once heard someone say we need to "delegate anxiety not just responsibility." Sometimes you get people to cooperate if you do not compromise your integrity as a leader. If you jump in the middle and cover for the mistakes of others, you end up consuming the responsibility and limiting the congregation's level of involvement. By sharing the anxiety, the burden ends up being shared by everyone rather than resting on the shoulders of a few frustrated individuals. This encourages cooperation and does not settle for compromise. People looking for a hot cup of coffee ended up realizing the need for shared responsibility. This continues to reveal how small things make a big difference, whether it is paying attention to ministry details or cleaning up our communication patterns.

Best Practice #3

The Internet and Direct Communication

Email and the Internet have enabled people to cooperate and collaborate on projects in many new ways. There are several sites that enable people to work on a single document simultaneously. There are even sign-up sheets that can be passed around your congregation online. We communicate through a variety of means including email and social networking sites. These resources enable pastors and church leaders to send clear and concise messages to ministry teams and a large percentage of the congregation all at once. Our church sends out a weekly email update called "The Email Connection" highlighting three to five things happening during the coming week. We also have attendance registry pads in our pews, and people can sign in and give us their names, addresses, and phone numbers if they are visitors. We have added a space to allow them to give us their email addresses if they want to receive weekly email announcements. Many first-time visitors give us their email addresses for this purpose. It is surprising to me how often visitors give us their email addresses before they give us their home addresses and phone numbers. These email addresses put us in direct contact with our visitors the week after they arrive, and this happens at their request. They also have a right and an avenue to unsubscribe.

One of the problems with email and social networking sites is that they can be both used and misused. For some reason, all the rules of etiquette in the real world go out the window with the Internet. People abbreviate words, fail to use capitalization, and often disregard grammar and spelling. However, the real problem is a failure to pay attention to common courtesies in communication. The "reply to all" button allows people to share personal information with large numbers of people in a conversation that should be taking place between two individuals. At times, people do not think about who should be getting the emails that they send. Before we hit the "reply to all" button, I think we should pause and think about to whom this email is being sent. Is the information you want to share appropriate for everyone on your list? Would you share this message verbally with the same group of people standing with you in a room? These are the kinds of questions we need to ask. Otherwise we can create dozens, if not hundreds, of triangles with just the push of a "reply to all" button, or an inappropriate post on a social networking site.

Church members occasionally copy their pastors on contentious emails they were sending to other church members. When they do this they are letting the pastor know that they are angry with someone, and indirectly asking the pastor to get involved with the relationship issue they have with this other person. These emails are indirectly inviting this pastor into a triangle. My advice is that pastors disregard these emails and wait for direct communication. If the person sharing this information asks why you are not responding, then simply say that you were not asked to. If it is a really contentious email, I might directly offer to facilitate a face-to-face discussion with the person who is angry. However, I would expect them to invite the other person to join us. The goal should always be open and direct communication between those involved. To achieve this, the clergy person should not take sides, but offer to facilitate communication.

Another disturbing act that I have observed in our use of the Internet is the broadcasting of personal messages that were delivered privately. One pastor friend of mine had a church member email her with a theological question on a controversial issue. This pastor sent this person a carefully worded response. The church member took this response and sent it to his brother, who was also a pastor, and it got a negative reaction. This person then broadcast that information to several other people in their church. This pastor friend of mine felt like she was being attacked by the church member. The real issue was not the theological debate, but the behavior of the church member who created multiple triangular relationships. He should not have taken information shared in a personal conversation and lifted it up for public evaluation without permission. If this pastor friend knew that she was posting something publically, then this would have been different. However, she did not post anything. She simply shared her point of view in a private email conversation. The sad thing is that trust was broken, and the relationship was damaged. It is easy to hurt people when we do not think about the consequences of our actions in relationship to the Internet. We all need to understand that common courtesy and appropriate behavior relates to our conversations in person and online.

chapter 4

Collaboration

Collaboration is the work we share directly with each other. It takes place when two or more people work together on a single project. Collaboration takes a high level of communication and teamwork. Through collaboration, we share authority, responsibility, and engagement. Three or more people can work collaboratively with each other on a specific project and not form any triangles. This requires open communication and clear opportunities for individuals to have an impact. Collaboration is time consuming and should be used in alignment with top priorities. Though it is often said "two heads are better than one," we cannot always devote two heads to every project. Therefore, it is important for staff teams and leadership bodies to determine which projects deserve the most amount of attention. Most churches have too many committees and meetings, but some committees can help a church to work more collaboratively together. Committees are most helpful when their responsibilities are clear and specific. They work best when they are asked to fulfill a specific task and when the committee is dissolved after the task is complete. In short, committees should be used as much as necessary, but as little as possible. You also want to use collaborative meetings wisely because of the amount of time and energy collaboration requires.

Priorities

In a book called *A Leader's Legacy*, Jim Kouzes and Barry Posner say that "A leader's legacy is really the legacy of many."[1] What they mean is that

1. Kouzes and Posner, *Legacy*, 45.

leadership is not all about us as individuals or our accomplishments. One of the things I have discovered as a pastor is that some of the best things that happen in the church under my leadership have very little to do with me. The best things that happen typically happen as a result of the space leaders offer to individuals and teams to develop and implement ministries. Ephesians 4:11–12 says, "The gifts he gave were that some would be apostles, some prophets, some evangelists, some pastors, and teachers, to equip the saints for the work of ministry, for building up the body of Christ." Pastors and staff in churches at times need to learn how to get out of the way of others. Our primary role is to equip the saints and to encourage collaboration among God's people.

One of my favorite examples of collaboration at our church in Massachusetts has to do with a ministry we started called the "Family Café." It all started when we had an adult education series on Sunday mornings focused on mission and outreach in our community. One of the speakers was a woman who is in charge of the "Food 'n Friends" kitchens. This group organizes traditional soup kitchens hosted by churches in our area. These kitchens mostly serve homeless or hungry individuals, and most of them are single men. The director of this program shared a concern about families after the economy crash in 2008 and her desire to see hungry and at-risk families served in a new way. The seed was planted in our adult Sunday school class, and the church people picked up on it. We utilized a steering committee to launch this new ministry of serving a meal once a month to families struggling to make their financial ends meet. This committee worked collaboratively to begin this ministry.

We named this ministry the "Food 'n Friends Family Café" and it is commonly known as the "Family Café." On the last Wednesday of every month, families with at least one child under eighteen years old are served a nutritious and well-balanced meal. This steering committee not only met to develop the initial plans, but it also met once a month after each "Family Café" to evaluate how things were going. One person was in charge of coordinating volunteers. Another was in charge of keeping the guest list and communicating with them each month. Two people share the meal planning and preparation. Still another person was in charge of ordering supplies and maintaining the kitchen. There were also many other volunteers who helped with setup, meal preparation, serving, and cleanup after the meal. It was teamwork at its best. We shared responsibility, but we also shared authority as the steering committee talked each month and made decisions.

We serve the meal restaurant style and have a craft corner for the children. I once heard a guest tell a person on the phone that she was at a restaurant. Another woman once said to a family member, "I am not used to being served." What started as a ministry in our church quickly became a ministry shared by other churches. Other churches in our community have begun serving these meals, as well. They, too, use the name "Family Café." The collaboration of our church members led to collaboration with other churches in the community. Now our community not only has traditional soup kitchens that serve hungry and homeless individuals, but we also have several "Family Cafés" that serve families in need. This is a clear example of something that was worthy of the time and energy it took for collaboration. Clearly it helps to utilize collaboration when you are launching a new ministry. Once a ministry is established, there is less need for conversation and decision-making and more room for cooperation.

One struggle many churches face is filling the positions they have on church boards and committees. In my book *Challenging the Church Monster: From Conflict to Community*, I wrote about the problem that many nominating committee's experience when they give people authority without responsibility.

> If nominating committees, desperate to fill vacancies within their overgrown church governments, promise minimal responsibility while freely giving authority to anyone willing to attend an occasional committee meeting, none of us should be surprised by the amount of conflict and anxiety embedded in our church systems.[2]

In this previous book, I focused on the problems that arise when we give people authority without responsibility. In this current book, I am suggesting that a different set of problems develop when we give people responsibility without authority. Giving people responsibility without authority leads people to feel like they are being taken advantage of or, at the very least, like they are being taken for granted. If we give people responsibility without authority, it makes them feel like they are not trusted—or even worse, that they cannot be trusted.

My brother once worked for a large corporation as a regional manager, and one of the top-level executives came to visit him at his plant and

2. Bixby, *Church Monster*, 59.

office. During the visit, my brother shared some of his ideas about the business. This executive leader responded, "Bixby, we do not pay you to think. We pay you to execute." In other words, he had been given responsibility, not authority. They wanted him to be productive but not to participate in the leadership. When you give people responsibility without any authority, it shows that you do not trust them, and it keeps people from feeling like they are a real part of a team. In this situation, my brother knew he was not calling the shots, but he also would have liked to have been heard. He was on the front lines of their business and was simply trying to share practical insights, not a global vision. Sharing authority does not mean letting go of the steering wheel. The executive leader needs to be the captain of the ship, and yet he or she does not always need the last word, or in this case every word. It is essential for leaders to at least listen to the ideas of others on the team.

Imagine if the captain of the *Titanic* had listened more carefully to the other people around him. Imagine how many lives would have been saved if he would have paid attention to the leaders who were trying to warn him about the iceberg that was in front of them. This captain obviously had more trust in the strength of his ship than he did the competence of the people around him. When you are the captain of a ship you are generally responsible for the ship and its direction. This, however, does not mean that you have to be behind every decision that gets made. Developing more cooperation and collaboration through listening allows a congregation to cultivate a culture of trust and togetherness. It helps leaders to make better decisions. This is why the senior pastor and leadership team should always remain open to input and to be willing to change direction when essential information is shared. When leaders share authority and responsibility with others it helps the leader with the coordination of everyone's effort. This type of sharing does not show weakness, but strength, and a willingness to work together as a team.

In a team environment, ideas can be shared freely, and all people included in discernment develop a high commitment to the overall success of these ministries. Working together is essential for effective ministry. When we work together we place a high level of priority on our ministries and relationships. Working together on our ministry goals helps to form the kind of community we hope to establish. When we share responsibility and authority freely, and when we make his mission our aim, there is no telling how effective our ministries can become. In the fifth chapter of Luke's gospel, we receive the story about the paralyzed man being lowered through a hole in a roof to bring him before Jesus. These friends took it upon themselves to do whatever it took to get this paralyzed person to Jesus. They cooperated and collaborated with each other to help. The goal should always be to serve God by serving others. It is about equipping people to follow through with ministry opportunities once they have clarity. When this kind of permission giving happens, we are truly providing the space needed for God and God's people to work together through the ministries of our churches.

Different Angles

When churches and staff teams become over-compartmentalized effective collaboration can be hard to achieve. I once consulted with an associate pastor in a church who was given the title "pastor to young adults." This was a church of 250 people. When a major conflict arose between the senior pastor and this associate pastor, one of the concerns raised was a lack of connection this associate pastor had with the older people in the church. The deeper hidden concern was the lack of connection the senior pastor was experiencing with the young adults. There seemed to be a clear division developing within the church, and the strange thing was that these lines were drawn by the title given to this new pastor long before the conflict even developed. This title put the new pastor in a silo and limited the impact he could have on the congregation as a whole.

When we give someone the title "pastor to young adults," we should not be surprised when age divisions occur. It is more constructive to refer to the pastor as a general associate and to simply divide the responsibilities behind the scenes through a structured but flexible job description. There is a difference between a division of labor in our job descriptions and the total compartmentalization of our responsibilities. For true teamwork to develop, the pastors and staff need to learn how to share ministry by sharing responsibility. We need to work together in a variety of ways in a collaborative environment. We should not build silos through job titles or job descriptions. Staff members may have specific roles and responsibilities, but they need to be able to lean on each other's strengths and to rely on each other's insights and participation.

One of my youth ministers and I used to talk a lot about collaboration in terms of doing ministry from different angles. I remember a complicated ministry situation arose with a high school student. The youth minister spoke with the student first. Then I ended up in a phone conversation with the parents. However, later that week I took the student out for lunch. Then during coffee hour after church, the youth minister had a conversation with the parents. One of the keys to ministering through different angles is respecting the communication process. When doing this type of ministry from different angles, both pastors should spend more time listening than speaking. If teamwork is to be possible in these highly personal and particularly challenging situations, then a high regard for confidentiality is essential. Neither the senior pastor nor the youth minister should share information that came from the student with the parents and vice versa.

It may seem easier to simply compartmentalize the relationships and say that the youth minister should talk to the students and the senior pastor should talk to the adults. But, I have always found that parents and students would talk to each of their two pastors about different aspects of their situation. For example, if a student has a well-known substance abuse problem and is arrested for possession of an illegal substance, then the goal for the staff is to talk with both the parents and the student about a way for them to deal with her drug problem. The senior pastor and the youth pastor may agree up front on the program path they want to encourage. This way the parents and the student are not getting mixed messages. It is important for the senior pastor and the youth pastor to be on the same page. If both the senior pastor and the youth pastor are on the same page, they can utilize the different angles in a positive direction.

Favoritism

One biblical example of how a spirit of competition leads into triangulation is the time the mother of James and John tried to negotiate for them with Jesus. She wanted to make sure her sons were treated favorably by Jesus in his kingdom. In Matthew 20:20–27 it says,

> Then the mother of the sons of Zebedee came to him with her sons, and kneeling before him, she asked a favor of him. And he said to her, "What do you want?" She said to him, "Declare that these two sons of mine will sit, one at your right hand and one at your left, in your kingdom." But Jesus answered, "You do not know what you are asking. Are you able to drink the cup that I am about to drink?" They said to him, "We are able." He said to them, "You will indeed drink my cup, but to sit at my right hand and at my left,

> this is not mine to grant, but it is for those for whom it has been prepared by my Father." When the ten heard it, they were angry with the two brothers. But Jesus called them to him and said, "You know that the rulers of the Gentiles lord it over them, and their great ones are tyrants over them. It will not be so among you; but whoever wishes to be great among you must be your servant, and whoever wishes to be first among you must be your slave; just as the Son of Man came not to be served but to serve, and to give his life a ransom for many.

In this case, we can see how the mother of the two boys got into the middle of the relationship between Jesus and her sons. This triangle also produced another triangle between the boys and the other disciples. It was a mess, and Jesus tried to navigate it with James and John. He ended up resolving it by talking about how Christ followers should utilize authority. He suggests that we do not use power to become tyrants who lord their authority over others, but servants who use their power to serve. He essentially points out that their mother was thinking in earthly terms, not in terms of the way the kingdom of God works. Then he says, "Even the Son of Man came not to be served, but to serve, and to give his life as a ransom for many." Once again, Jesus used a triangle as a teachable moment for his disciples.

Fear

Church leadership is not about getting other people to do what you want them to do. Leadership in the church is about providing the space for people to work together in accordance with God's priorities. Collaboration demands a high level of communication. There is a big difference between three people working together on a project and three people entering into a triangular relationship. Three people can work on one project without emotional triangles. This, however, is not to say that three people working together are not vulnerable to triangulation. One pastor I know learned a valuable lesson in this regard when he was working on a small task force in his church. This task force was preparing a new website for their congregation. They decided to keep the process simple by having only three people on the task force. The two church members brought the technical knowledge, and the pastor was responsible for developing most of the content. The pastor was excited about the project and the small group approach. However, he found that he was having a hard time communicating with the two other people involved. He was trying to avoid triangulation by emailing one person at a time. Then he realized that this tactic was actually leading them into the triangles he was trying to avoid.

This pastor confessed that when they were starting this project, he did not always send emails to both of his partners because he was trying to have more control. The pastor was trying to avoid discussing a particular issues with one or the other person on the team. He was avoiding open and transparent communication because he was afraid one of them would want to take control and lead the group in a direction he did not want to go. This restricted communication was limiting their ability to function as a team. The lesson he learned was that there is a big difference between avoiding triangulation and avoiding difficult discussions. In this case, the "reply to all" button was a friend, not a foe. This pastor eventually discovered the need to consistently share the same information with both of his partners. This experience made him realize it was difficult to collaborate with two other people, but it was still possible. He eventually started including everyone in the group on each one of his emails and they were able to effectively complete the project. The website was well organized, colorful, and filled with pictures and pertinent information.

One way to emotionally gauge if you are trying to avoid open communication is if you feel like you are trying to sneak something through the system. This pastor was clearly doing this at first and realized that he needed to change. If this pastor was truly trying to collaborate at the beginning of the project, he would have been more willing to have difficult discussions about the project all along the way. He failed to trust the others enough and he became controlling, rather than collaborative. This breakdown in communication was the result of fear. He was afraid to trust the process and the people with whom he was working. Then he realized that if this team was going to function effectively, they all needed to be totally open and honest with each other. All three people on the project were filling different roles. However, all three needed to be on the same page with regard to the single direction they were heading. Collaboration takes effort and communication requires patience. The question for any group project is, "Are you willing to do the hard work of making decisions together?" Once the people in this group became more transparent the decision-making got easier. They cooperated and collaborated with each other and the project ended up being a success.

Blame

Blame is the foundation of many difficulties within congregational systems. If you are a leader who is constantly looking for ways to blame others, then you will eventually be swimming in a sea of triangles. Conflict will bubble up all around you, and it will at times consume you. When someone is complaining to me about another church leader, I first try to encourage the person complaining to talk directly with the leader themselves. Sometimes, however, the things people get upset about are minor issues, and it is easier for me to simply take the blame. Taking the blame in conflict situations can help the people in our congregations to avoid unnecessary conflicts. Most issues that arise in church life are not very big issues, but the behavior of leaders make the issues out to be bigger than they are. This is why one of my favorite things to say in a contentious conversation is "this was probably my fault." I like to apologize for the things I can apologize for whenever I can. Apologizing makes conflict less enjoyable for troublemakers and troubled people. Apologies kill much of the contentiousness within these conversations, especially if a disgruntled person is trying to blame someone else on your staff and to drag you into the middle of it.

If we join in blaming every issue on someone other than ourselves, we will tear away at the fabric of the relationships that make up the church community. When we blame others for problems in the church we set ourselves up for a life of triangulation. Nothing fosters triangulation and miscommunication like blame. Church leaders who want to improve communication and build a sense of community refuse to play the blame game. As a senior pastor, I have come to the conclusion that I can do a lot of damage by blaming my staff or other church leaders for problems that emerge. As the head of staff, it makes sense for me to bear as much responsibility as I can. This does not mean that we should allow other members of our staff team to avoid responsibility. It simply means that we do not have to include all the people who are complaining about a particular issue in the problem solving. If key leaders simply take the blame up front, then problems can be solved more methodically inside appropriate staff and leadership contexts. Avoiding the blame game helps leaders to navigate the nonsense more effectively, and it leads to better communication patterns and a higher level of connection with your church people.

Some pastors feel like they are blamed for everything bad that happens in their church. This often leads them into a defensive posture. Taking the blame early in your tenure is an offensive move and this can keep you from developing a defensive posture. If the leaders in your church stop running around trying to figure out who to blame for problems, they may actually run around trying to figure out how to resolve problems. If the complaining and blaming in your church is minimized, trust will be established, and a clear sense of community will begin to emerge. No one likes being blamed and it does not always feel natural to take the blame, but I typically find it is more helpful to take the blame than it is to cast it. Taking the blame typically keeps "mole hills" from turning into "mountains." Taking the blame and working with your team to resolve issues may also help leaders to take more advantage of the ministry opportunities that are before them.

Consequences

While I was in Connecticut we called our second youth minister. He was a graduate of North Park University, and we called him right out of college into youth ministry. The first weekend Ben was at our church he had a bonfire for our high school students on our church grounds. The fire was not the problem. The problem was that he decided to play games with the students based on a reality television show that made people eat things that were difficult to swallow. Among other things, he fed two of our students a can of dog food during this game. These students were brothers and happened to mention this culinary experience to their parents. The parents had just recently joined the church. Needless to say this did not go over too well with them. It also raised some questions in the minds of a few of our church members and leaders. There are times when taking the blame as the head of staff is not a good idea. Sometimes other pastors, staff members, and lay leaders need to be responsible for the consequences of their actions.

To be honest, I did not try to protect Ben in the midst of this situation. I did not take the blame. I let him bear the responsibility for his actions. I pointed every upset person I could to Ben's office. He created this mess, and I wanted him to know that he would be the one to clean it up. I wanted him to realize that he was now the authority figure who would have to be responsible for the outcome of his actions. He was in a job where he needed to make the rules, not break them. I wanted this dog food experience to be a learning opportunity for him, and I discovered that the best way to do this was to simply stay out of the middle. I knew that he was strong enough to handle this. Ben and I talked extensively about this situation after the fact. He came to me quite flustered and asked, "What do I do?" We talked about why it was important to develop trust with the parents, and how it was important to have good relationships with both the adults and the kids at our church.

If I tried to protect Ben from the reaction of these parents, then I would have been in the middle, and he could have played the role of the victim. Staying out of the middle forced Ben to take responsibility, and he ended up learning a lot from this experience. Ben ended up having a very positive relationship with both the students and the parents at our church. His relationship with the family whose kids ate the dog food was especially strong. Avoiding the middle in this situation forced him to be accountable to these others. This helped his relationships to develop more thoroughly. It gave him the opportunity to take responsibility, to develop positive relationships with the people in our church, and to grow in his identity as a minister. He was a great youth pastor, and he cared deeply for our students. I recently had an opportunity to attend his ordination service, and now he is serving as a lead pastor.

Protection

Taking responsibility as a leader is one clear way toward improving communication in any organization. Sometimes people get angry with the triangulating behavior of others. They focus more on others than themselves. When they do this they often fail to focus enough on how they are contributing to the communication problems. The best way to limit the impact of triangulation within our congregations is by focusing on our personal actions and taking responsibility for ourselves. Even when people say or do things that set us up for emotional triangles, we need to avoid saying and doing the things that further connect the dots and complete the triangles. It is more productive to focus on ourselves in this regard than it is to focus on the role of the other in these triangular experiences. When person A talks to you about person B then you must resist sharing this information with person B. This can be hard to do and it can be tempting to blame person A for starting the triangle. Encouraging person A to talk directly with person B is your primary goal. Keeping yourself from sharing the information from person A with person B is your leadership responsibility. This has to do with keeping ourselves from completing triangles as a way of managing conflict.

One senior pastor I worked with told me about a situation that developed with her staff of three other full-time staff. In this situation, two staff members had been talking negatively about the senior pastor during a coffee break and the third staff member heard it. His name was Steven. Steven was concerned about this negativity and shared what he observed with the senior pastor. The senior pastor confronted the two other staff members who were complaining about her. She said that if you have concerns, speak directly to me. She was right. However, the problem was that she now created new triangles between Steven and the two other staff members. Steven was now the one who told on them and in their eyes he could not be trusted. You can see how this situation would continue to escalate and erode any trust levels that remained in the relationships on their staff team. At first glance, it appears that Steven was trying to be helpful. Steven was trying to protect the senior pastor. Nevertheless, this person was also in the best position to minimize the amount of triangulation taking place.

When I was a child, we would have called this person a "tattletale" in our neighborhood. You see the "tattler" could have let the issues these other staff people had with the senior pastor escalate on their own. He did not need to get in the middle. He did not need to report this information to the senior pastor. Steven could have encouraged the other staff members to talk directly with the senior pastor about their concerns. In my mind, Steven is the one the senior pastor should have confronted. She could have used this as an opportunity to coach Steven about triangulation. Steven was striving to be loyal to the senior pastor, but his behavior was leaving an indelible mark on the staff relationships. As senior pastors we do not need other people to protect us. We do not need staff members who feel responsible for solving all our problems. If we expect another staff member to play the role of rescuing us, then they will end up in the middle. Senior pastors in large churches should see all their staff members as allies. The last thing you want to develop on a staff team are sides. This will lead into devastating consequences.

The protectors among us are actually in a very good position to keep relationship triangles from taking shape. The temptation to protect must be resisted in order to avoid triangles. Those of us trying to protect everyone else in this world seem to create a lot of triangles. We like to appear helpful. We like to be the hero. However, we need to learn how to stay out of the middle and let other people's problems unfold naturally. We also need to encourage difficult discussions. When we enter into relationship triangles, we are typically trying to help, but we actually end up hurting. The irony is that most of the issues we are trying to protect each other from are not really all that threatening. Most of us have the capacity to deal with difficult conversations. This is why protectors need to recognize that the other adults around them can handle themselves and their situations. There is typically no need for superheroes as we seek to navigate the nonsense.

Momentum

A friend of mine was recently called to serve as one of the pastors in a large, growing, urban, multiethnic congregation. It is a young congregation, both in terms of the age of its members and the number of years it has been in existence. They clearly have more weddings than funerals. This friend of mine had a strong reputation in youth ministry. He was typically called into older, established churches to establish a new level of energy and momentum. The interesting thing about the call extended from this church is that they wanted him because of his experience, and they saw him as someone who could help stabilize their ministries. They called him because of who he was, not because of anything specific they needed him to do. They actually created a new position for him just to bring him on board. His job description has changed dramatically on a regular basis ever since. The congregation clearly sees him as one of the pastors of their church, but my guess is that few people would know how to define his position. He clearly has a flexibly structured job description. The thing I love about this is that they are using his gifts and abilities in a variety of very profound ways. They have allowed him to help in the places that needed help. He has helped in the areas of outreach, youth ministry, men's ministry, worship leading, retreats, and adult discipleship.

Erwin Raphael McManus wrote a book called *The Unstoppable Force: Daring to Become the Church God Had in Mind.* In this book he writes,

> When I talk to pastors and church leaders, I rarely find people who do not have it in their hearts to touch the world with the love of Christ. Often the exact opposite is true. Many are followers of Jesus who are deeply burdened with the human condition. They care deeply about what God cares about; they understand that Jesus came to seek and save that which is lost; they know their churches should relevantly and powerfully impact the world around them;

> but they just can't seem to get across the street. Unseen obstacles keep knocking them down. It's hard to gain momentum when, every time you pick up speed you crash into something.[3]

My theory is that many of the obstacles we crash into are emotional triangles. These triangles stunt our congregational growth and the keep us from effectively serving our communities as we ought to. The reason I think avoiding triangulation is so important is because indirect communication can limit your ability to minister effectively. I believe direct communication can help us do a better job of reaching out because you are less entangled in the web of miscommunication that often complicates ministries.

The friend I just mentioned is very gifted and creative guy, and he was called to serve within a very creative and collaborative setting. He always dreamed about being a part of a staff team like this. He never wanted to be in the lead position. He wanted to be a part of something that was larger than himself. In some ways, he was called to collaborate with the other pastors and staff at this church. This led him to become a stabilizing force and a productive member of the team. Some churches would have a hard time being this flexible, but I believe that all pastors should be called to be collaborators. It does not matter what the position title is or how your job description says it, but collaboration with the other pastors, staff, and the leaders of your church should be a part of your responsibility in any congregation. Church leaders need to do a better job of making space for the collaborative efforts of its leaders. What I am saying is that collaboration should become an expectation, not a dream, for our churches.

Best Practice #4

Education about Triangulation

Teaching about triangulation is key to implementing a comprehensive approach to encouraging "direct communication." In both of my churches, I have utilized leadership orientation meetings as a primary and consistent way to teach church leaders about this. We hold these meetings once a year, the week after our annual meeting in January. The annual meeting is the time when our new leaders and officers are elected. At the leadership orientation meeting, we go over triangulation and talk about how to avoid it.

3. McManus, *Unstoppable Force*, 41.

Church leaders are encouraged to do three things if a disgruntled church member talks with them about a conflict. The first step is to listen. Sometimes people simply need to vent their emotions. They talk about the issues and feel better because they were able to discuss what they were upset about. The second step is to encourage direct communication. If the person is upset with someone in particular, then the leader should encourage them to have this difficult discussion. If the individual is too anxious, then the leader can offer to go with them during the difficult discussion. The leader may even be able to help set up the conversation.

I have emphasized avoiding triangulation at these orientation meetings once a year since I began in ministry twenty years ago, and I have never heard a person complain about the repetition. People actually enjoy hearing about this because it reveals a simple method for navigating the nonsense. It gives your church leaders confidence that there is a way to keep conflict from escalating, and it keeps anxiety levels in the church low. Trust levels escalate and miscommunication patterns deteriorate. I also strive to model this behavior on a daily basis in my own life and ministry. I seek to educate my staff and church leaders about triangulation privately through personal conversations. In my staff relationships we talk about our success and failures with this on a regular basis. As pastors and leaders we need to set an example for others, and we at times need to come alongside others to help them with direct communication.

One of my colleagues tells a story about clearing up a communication catastrophe in his church. Their music director was having solo auditions for the kids in their Junior Choir. Several students showed up for the auditions, but only a few kids got solos. One parent called this friend of mine concerned about the fact that her child did not get a solo. She thought that this type of audition was too high-pressured for young kids. Internally, my friend agreed with this and thought the music director could have handled it in a better way. However, he did the right thing and encouraged this parent to speak directly with the music director. He even asked this mother if she would feel more comfortable if he were there to meet with them. The mother said yes, and the music director later agreed with the plan. This pastor told both of them that he would simply be there to help facilitate the conversation.

When the meeting took place, he ended up being a silent partner in the room. He told me that he just sat there and listened as the two of them talked it out. The mother shared her concerns, and then our music director explained that her policy was that anyone who auditions for a solo gets a solo eventually. The parent explained that it would have helped if she told the kids that. The music director agreed and apologized, and a major conflict was resolved. Most of the time, these challenging conversations can take place without the support of a third person. However, in this situation, it helped everyone to feel more comfortable when the pastor came alongside them. This type of leadership allows a person to stay out of the middle without seeming aloof or uninvolved. The best way for clergy to teach this to lay leaders is by modeling it. It also helps if senior pastors are willing to receive this kind of help from lay leaders.

To help make this happen senior pastors need to give lay leaders permission to offer to facilitate difficult discussions for them with disgruntled members. These leaders need to know that you see this kind of assistance as helpful, not hurtful, even if they are emotional and difficult conversations. If pastors do not give their lay leaders permission to do this, then they will inevitably be anxious about suggesting it. Their fear is that they will be seen as an instigator of the issues, when in reality they are just bringing them into the light. Nine times out of ten, I find most difficult conversations simply clear up confusion and help to resolve problematic issues. There is a clear difference between coming alongside someone in a conflict situation and entering into the middle. The interesting thing is that I find most conflict in the church is manageable when you seek to deal with it directly on a regular basis. Again, it is not about avoiding conflict, but avoiding triangles.

Some churches employ "behavioral covenants" or "relational covenants" as a way to ensure that people are talking *to each other* and not *about each other* in conflict situations. These are publically stated congregational agreements to behave in a particular way in the midst of conflict. I have never felt the need to use a behavioral covenant. I simply teach direct communication as the way we do things. I love it when someone in my church begins a conversation saying, "I know I am triangling you, but . . . ." This helps me to know that they are at least aware of these kind of communication patterns. At a performance review after my third year in Attleboro, the reviewer spoke about conflict management and said that my approach of "avoiding triangulation helps immensely." When the people in your church know about triangulation and direct communication on this level, it shows that this practice has begun to offer shape to the congregational culture. This culture shift helps you to navigate the nonsense more effectively.

ZONE III: HIGHER ELEVATIONS

The top floor of tall buildings is often treated with dignity. Executive suites in corporate offices tend to be on the top floor. The top floor of a resort hotel is the honeymoon suite. The top floor in a business hotel is the executive suite. The top floor of an apartment building is the penthouse. There is a famous scene on a top floor balcony in the movie *Pretty Woman* where Richard Gere reveals he is afraid of heights, and Julia Roberts asks him why he stays on the top floor. He responds, "Because it's the best." Churches that have the best communication patterns hover between creativity and community. This is why I call this level of communication the higher elevations. Zone three churches are churches that make ministry and church life seem effortless. Communication is clear, and ministry is very effective. People know how to stay out of each other's way, and they know how to care for each other in crisis situations. No church is perfect, but churches that experience these higher elevations have found a secure place outside of the basement. These churches work smarter, not just harder. The trust within their systems allows them to deal with conflict effectively and this gives rise to the kind of cooperation and collaboration that makes room for a lot of creativity and community.

chapter 5

Creativity

Most people tend to think about creativity as an individual endeavor. We think about a potter on a wheel, a painter with a brush, or a composer at a keyboard. But creativity is actually something that emerges from relationships. Creativity is the work we do that allows us to leave our fingerprints on the world. Creativity in our churches and organizations stems from the kind of cooperation and collaboration that allows individuals and groups to fully express their ideas and to make significant contributions. Creativity develops when individuals are allowed to think beyond the limits of their current circumstances and where positive relational environments allow good ideas to flourish. Creativity is fun, and it often produces great ministry results. When a community experiences low trust levels and many layers of triangulation then creativity is impaired. Creativity is particularly limited in a basement environment that hovers between conflict and compromise. On the other hand, if the communication on your team hovers between cooperation and collaboration, then creativity will inevitably be cultivated. Some creativity can emerge from a crisis or a conflict, but typically it flows more freely from a place where cooperation and collaboration are the norm.

Creativity is often inspired by our relationships and the issues in them. The songs people write are often inspired by the pain or joy experienced in human relationships. The paintings artists produce often express emotions or ideas that have something to do with relationships. The same could be said about a choreographed dance. People and relationships also impact our creativity directly. We could all name teachers, coworkers, spouses, mentors, and friends who have influenced our creative efforts, both directly and indirectly. When people work closely together and allow ideas to bounce off each other, creativity emerges. This is why a positive working environment allows creative ideas to flourish. Creativity has to do with looking at a problem from many angles or seeing something that is possible and stretching it in a variety of different directions. This sharing of creative ideas requires courage and trust. Creativity emerges in our preaching, teaching, and program leadership. When triangles are minimized our pastors and leaders are more focused and creative.

Hope

Congregations that hope to become more creative effectively allow space for dreams to develop and visions to be cast. In my first year of pastoral ministry, I inadvertently turned a budget meeting into a vision meeting. I asked the people planning our budget to begin their time together by imagining what it would be like if we had twice as much money to spend in the year that was before us. I asked them to dream a little. This frustrated some people, but it inspired others. No one took it too seriously, but we had fun exploring ideas and thinking outside the box. It was in this meeting that the idea to have a youth minister first emerged. Some thought this exercise was crazy because they could not imagine the budget being twice the size, and they saw this exercise as a waste of valuable time. The interesting thing is that ten years later, the budget had more than doubled, and we had a full-time youth minister. This was a church that once considered going to a part-time pastor. They now had two full-time ministers. If a vision had not been established and communicated, who knows what would have happened? Proverbs 29:18 says, "Where there is no vision, the people will perish."

One of my daughters recently finished taking a driver's education course. This course began with a meeting between the teachers and the parents. One of the things the program director told us was that they would teach our kids was to aim high with their eyes. He said many student drivers get into trouble when they consistently look down at the bumper or the brake lights of the car in front of them. He said that if they aim high with their eyes, then they will not only see the brake lights of the car in front of them but also the activity of vehicles and pedestrians beyond that car and along the sides of the road before them. I do not remember being taught to aim high with my eyes when I learned to drive, but I clearly do this as an experienced driver. It is amazing how much more you see when you keep your head up and your eyes focused forward. To be a good driver you have to be aware of what is going on in front of you and around you. To be a good leader in the church, you cannot only respond to urgent matters as they arise, you must also look further down the road and assess what will need to be cultivated in the future.

The main reason senior pastors need a clear vision for their ministries is that a clear vision allows leaders to stay focused on the future even after difficulties arise. Vision allows pastors to aim high with their eyes and to keep their heads above water in challenging times. It allows them to lead strategically in the midst of all the particular challenges and bumps in the road during their church experiences. It also helps churches to cultivate creativity in their ministries. Many pastors have lost positions or left the ministry because of conflict situations that escalated and became all-consuming. When this happens the conflict is all they seem to be aware of, it is as if they only see the brake lights in front of them. This makes navigating the nonsense very difficult. It is hard to trust a leader who cannot see beyond their immediate circumstances. People struggle to follow a leader who does not have hope for the future of their church or organization, especially when conflict or controversy is present.

Vision

I encourage pastors in a new call to write a twenty-year scenario during the first few weeks of their ministries. This is an opportunity for lead pastors to look down the road and creatively imagine what their churches could look like in this future. Casting this kind of vision helps pastors because it allows them to see beyond their immediate circumstances. It also allows churches to believe that things can be different in the future. There is typically a grace period given to pastors when they first get started. They are able to aim high with their eyes for at least a few weeks. This allows the clergy person to dream big about the future without much interference. Eventually, budget shortfalls, program challenges, and conflict issues start to take over and make vision casting more difficult. Once this grace period passes, church leaders want their pastors to join them in focusing on the immediate concerns including practical realities and fiscal challenges.

While preparing a twenty-year scenario, you can write about changes in your facilities, your staff, your membership, your programs, number of services, style of worship, your approach to ministry, the way your people relate to one another, and the way you function in general. The great thing about a twenty-year scenario is that you can dream big without scaring anyone. The older people in your church will not feel threatened because they do not expect to be here twenty years from now, and the young adults in your church have no idea what will take place in their lives over this twenty-year period. Therefore, it is not very threatening to dream big when what you are dreaming about something that is far away. Some people will not take your dream too seriously because of this, but other people will begin to wonder why some of the things in your vision statement couldn't happen now. They begin to see what you are dreaming about as an immediate possibility.[1]

I wrote twenty-year scenarios in both Connecticut and Massachusetts during my first few weeks in each location. One of the things I did at both of my churches to prepare the twenty-year scenarios was to develop focus group meetings with church members in my first few weeks. These were small groups of people with anyone who wanted to talk with me about what they wanted to see happen over the next several years. People signed up to come and talk with me. I met with groups of four to twelve people. Whoever signed up during the times I made available came and shared their thoughts and feelings with me. I asked them to share their stories about how they came to the church. I also asked them to speak about what they valued most in the church and what their hopes and dreams were for the congregation. In both locations, the people who came said that they wanted the church to grow in terms of size, togetherness, and outreach. These focus group meetings helped me to establish a vision that was based on their desires and what they believed God expected from them. These vision statements were written by me, but they grew out of these conversations.

Through the twenty-year scenario a senior pastor can show their congregation that they believe in the church and a God who can help make all these things happen. After ten years in Connecticut, a long-term member of my church, who tended to be a bit cynical, told me that he laughed when he first read my first twenty-year scenario. He said, "I never believed any of it was possible." Then he said, "Now it all has happened." The thing I realized about this man's experience was that he initially did not believe in the possibility of any change. Then when he saw that some things changed

1. I first learned about the twenty-year scenario at North Park Theological Seminary in 1992, in a leadership class taught by Walter C. Wright.

he began to believe that everything had. He laughed at first because he did not believe things could be different. At the same time, he saw a leader who believed things could. Even though he initially did not take the vision statement seriously, a seed of hope had been planted. I came to realize the vision statement showed him that at least one person believed in God's power to transform the church, and in the fact that God's people could help make it happen.

Implementation

After two years in Attleboro, I met with a group of leaders from our congregation who felt that I was being a little too creative. Their fear was that I might be introducing too many new programs and ideas. I did not react negatively to this because I understood what they were saying. I had, in fact, introduced a significant number of new programs, including small groups and fellowship dinner groups. These were programs that were successful in my previous setting. These folks feared the creativity would never stop. The fear was that the congregation would have a tough time keeping up with all of these new ideas. In this meeting, I told everyone that they had nothing to worry about because I had already used up all of my good ideas. Though I said it in jest, there was an element of truth to it. I utilized some of the creative work I had done in the past to benefit my current church, but future creativity would depend more on the collective effort of the church membership.

Introducing a significant number of programs in a short period of time may have given people the impression that other people's ideas would not be considered in the future. The truth is that all pastors need the creativity of others around them. Creativity is clearly a group effort, however, one of the problems I have discovered with creativity is that good ideas typically require valuable resources. Good ideas typically take up time, energy, and finances when they are being implemented. It is important to realize this as we discuss the good ideas that are generated. When introducing something new, we not only need to think about the change itself, but also the amount of time and energy that will be required. I think this is why our leaders were wondering if I was being a little too creative. You cannot share an unlimited number of ideas that require the time and energy of other people, so you need to learn how to share new ideas at an appropriate pace. You also need to discern which ideas are really worth investing in. All congregations have a limited amount of resources. Creativity must be utilized as we seek to maximize the impact of the stewardship of these resources within our communities.

In her book *Pursuing God's Will Together*, Ruth Haley Barton writes, "Discernment together as leaders takes us beyond the personal to an increasing capacity to 'see' what God is up to in the place we are called to lead."[2] In congregational discernment, it is most helpful to identify the difference between discerning God's will and defending our personal preferences. While there is nothing wrong with personal preferences, congregational discernment is more about God's will for the congregation than it is the majority opinion. When we understand what God is up to, we become more trusting, and we begin to lay the groundwork for better communication patterns. There are times when the easiest thing for churches to do is compromise when there is a major difference of opinion. We choose compromise instead of having the difficult discussion needed to make a difficult decision. Creativity requires commitment to courageously pursue God's will within your congregation.

Betrayal

Jesus must have been a little confused when Judas betrayed him. How could one of his twelve betray him? How could he do this after all that Jesus had done for them and all that they had been through together? How was this even possible? In Luke 22:47–53 it says:

> While Jesus was still speaking, suddenly a crowd came, and the one called Judas, one of the twelve, was leading them. He approached Jesus to kiss him; but Jesus said to him, "Judas, is it with a kiss that you are betraying the Son of Man?" When those who were around him saw what was coming, they asked, "Lord, should we strike with the sword?" Then one of them struck the slave of the high priest and cut off his right ear. But Jesus said, "No more of this!" And he touched the ear and healed him. Then Jesus said to the chief priests, the offices of the temple police, and the elders who had come for him, "Have you come out with swords and clubs as if I were a bandit? When I was with you day after day in the temple, you did not lay hands on me. But this is your hour, and the power of darkness."

2. Barton, *Pursuing God's Will*, 20.

One of the beautiful things about the way Jesus handled this situation with Judas was his refusal to let others protect him by fighting back on his behalf. He did not want to treat Judas or these religious leaders like enemies, even though they had betrayed him. Jesus spoke directly to Judas and said, "Judas, is it with a kiss that you are betraying the Son of Man?" Jesus also insinuates that he is surprised that the religious leaders were treating him in this way. He firmly points out how they did not treat him this way in the temple.

When Jesus confronted Judas and the religious leaders, this was direct communication at its best, and his refusal to let his disciples fight back was another way he refused triangulation. I think the situation with Judas made Jesus feel sad, but his understanding of the human condition allowed Jesus to confront Judas graciously with a challenging question. We need to recognize that when Jesus was betrayed by Judas, he did not betray himself or the integrity of his relationships with the other people involved. Churches are not places where we should categorize people as "enemies" and "allies." Sometimes it feels like people are against you on a particular issue, but this does not make them an enemy. In church leadership, we need to make sure that people feel like they matter to us no matter what side of an issue they are on. It is best to treat everyone in the congregation as an ally. If we treat others like they are insignificant simply because of their personal preferences on a particular matter, then we may inadvertently be adding fuel to the conflicts that are burning beneath the surface within our relationships. Forming alliances with some and distance with others in the church allows these others to behave like enemies and this ends up being destructive.

Challenge

I had a very wise and gracious Old Testament professor at North Park Seminary named Fred Holmgren. He not only had expertise with regard to the Hebrew Bible, but he was also sensitive to the leadership challenges that new pastors would face in the church. He tried to prepare us for these leadership challenges. The mantra he taught us was, "Don't say too much, and don't say too little." He was encouraging us to use wisdom and to practice discernment through these simple words. He said this so often in class that we would sometimes joke about it with him. The funny thing, however, is that it always stuck with me. This mantra has helped me to navigate the nonsense for over twenty years of ministry. I often pause when writing an email, responding to a post on Facebook, or presenting a creative idea, and say these words: "Don't say too much, and don't say too little." Avoiding change for the sake of avoiding conflict often leads churches into a state of stagnation and decline. The fear of instability or a disequilibrium keeps us from presenting creative ideas. One of the leadership responsibilities we have in any church is making sure that there is enough instability to allow for creativity. Without change the church will also not experience enough movement for momentum to be established. Things have to feel a little crazy and confusing sometimes if you want your church to be a church that experiences momentum.

Sometimes in the church we try things, and they fail. Sometimes we do not try things because we are afraid they are going to fail. Our aim should always be progress, not perfection. Sometimes our creative ideas are well received, but other times they are not. We need to be prepared for conflict in this realm of creativity, and we should not be afraid of it. Change and conflict often go hand in hand. If you have too much change or too much stability, then you are not going to experience momentum. This is where avoiding conflict at all cost can be detrimental. All churches need a certain amount of change and instability to remain healthy. Creativity often leads into change, and change tends to lead into conflict. If churches have enough creativity, then they will also experience some conflict. If there is no conflict, then there may not be enough creativity. Most people do not like substantial change, and they clearly avoid too much conflict. This is why church people react negatively when there is too much creativity. The key for congregational vitality is understanding the need for some creativity and conflict to remain healthy.

In his book *A Failure of Nerve: Leadership in the Age of the Quick Fix,* Edwin Friedman writes about the stress of being a leader.

> Trying to be creative and imaginative is stressful, being responsible is stressful, maintaining vision is stressful, being on the lookout for and trying to deal with sabotage is stressful.[3]

Friedman clearly recognizes the challenge of leadership in the age of quick fixes and simple solutions. None of us likes change, stress, or conflict, but we need it to keep moving forward and to stay alive. Churches need to find creative ways to respond to the ministry challenges and leadership opportunities. Creativity is something that grows out of collaboration.

3. Friedman, *Failure of Nerve*, 220.

Collaboration happens when individuals work together. When we work together and share ideas, new ideas flourish. Creativity grows out of the work we do together over long periods of time.

I had a conversation with a youth pastor who had only been in his church for one year. It was a church with a very active youth ministry, and he was following someone who had been in his position for more than a decade. He was feeling anxious because several parents said that their children were not feeling as connected as they used to feel within their youth ministries. This young man was a very capable leader and doing everything he possibly could to sustain and strengthen the youth ministries. I encouraged him to see this lack of connection as a part of the transition. I asked him if he felt connected to the people of the church yet. He said, "No, not really." We talked about how he would have to start feeling more connected with the church before the students would begin feeling connection with the youth ministries. Building this kind of interconnectedness is what you are after in any ministry and it does not happen overnight. This kind of connection takes time to develop.

One church I was working with was having a hard time retaining their first-time visitors. They saw themselves as friendly but their visitors were not returning regularly. One of the members of this church had a creative idea and shared it with the pastor. The program was called "bread for visitors." This church member started baking a loaf of bread for every first-time visitor to the church. She placed it in a decorative bag and brought it to the home of anyone who left their address on one of their attendance pads. After a while other people in the church started helping with the baking, the bags, and the delivery. It was a great idea that flourished within their congregation. It also helped them to improve the retention of first-time visitors. No one in this situation sought to blame others for their failure to retain visitors. This woman simply offered a creative response that helped to solve a significant problem.

Change

My good friend Judy Peterson is the Campus Pastor at North Park University. She was recently the speaker at a clergy retreat I attended at Pilgrim Pines Conference Center in New Hampshire. At this retreat she spoke about the challenge of being a pastor. She said that all pastors need "thick skin" and "tender hearts." The problem, she said, is that many of us have developed "thin skin" and "hard hearts." These comments rang true to many to us. The reason they rang true is because the leadership we are called to do as pastors is difficult. She was talking about the pain that is associated with being a pastor, and the sacrifices we are asked to make in order to provide significant leadership. The need for "thick skin" and "tender hearts" is especially true for pastors in the midst of church conflict or significant change.[4]

Sometimes leaders need to be willing to disrupt the equilibrium of our congregations. We need to allow change to happen even when it feels uncomfortable. Change often allows momentum to emerge. When we embrace a more adventurous approach to being the church, we will make some mistakes. None of us are perfect and not all of our ideas are going to work. However, we should never give up on our hope of making things better for the churches that we serve. We need to try new things, experiment with new opportunities, and undertake all kinds of risks and adventures together. Most established churches are not this agile or adventurous. So even if a new adventure fails, positive results can ripple off of that adventure regardless of an apparent disruption. The long-term implications of a period of instability can help to reframe the future of a particular area of ministry or for your congregation.

Most churches are not prepared for substantive change until after the third year of a pastor's tenure. Avoiding triangles and practicing direct communication can have a deep level of impact during the "trust verses mistrust" time period. For one reason or another, churches believe that you have to make it through your first few conflict situations before they will allow you to introduce substantive change. This is why patience and persistence are essential as you begin leading your church. The key is not giving up when conflict arises in the first three years. If you do give up or give into the volatility, then they will not trust you with the difficult task of providing creative leadership.

The good news is that once these patterns of communication are established and a high level of trust is cultivated, there is plenty of room for creativity. When first-call pastors become discouraged during their first few years, then it is always wise to tell them about the "trust verses mistrust" stage. This three-year marker can give a new pastor hope, which is an essential foundation for the patience and the persistence he or she will need. Many things change after a church decides to trust a pastor's leadership.

4. Judy Peterson made these presentations at the 2013 East Coast Conference Minister's Retreat at Pilgrim Pines Conference Center in Swanzey, New Hampshire.

They not only allow you to lead but also to introduce substantive change. It may be that congregations utilize this "trust verses mistrust" period to see if a pastor's skin is thick enough and their heart tender enough for effective ministry. Once a church decides that the pastor is worthy of this trust it is amazing how flexible and experimental these congregations can become. New life and spiritual transformation become the norm for congregations that embrace such new beginnings.

BEST PRACTICE #5

Overall Ministry Review

Another tool I have used to talk about vision in the past is "a big picture meeting." Sometimes church leaders who are focused on governance become preoccupied with details and budget issues. This is particularly true if your finances are in trouble. Focusing on numbers and money every month in your meetings is one clear way to make sure that your vision will remain on the back burner. All you see are the brake lights in front of you. Occasional big picture meetings can help your governing body focus entirely on the future. At a "big picture" meeting you invite your leaders to think outside of the box and begin dreaming about what it would be like if current limitations were not holding the church back. You can also do this with your entire congregation. A good friend of mine calls his big picture congregational gatherings "town meetings." At these meetings, he gives his church members the opportunity to dream out loud about the future of their congregation.

Performance reviews in our church use to feel preoccupied with minutia, but lately they have allowed us to focus on the big picture. This started happening a few years ago when we restructured our review process. Previously within our system, a committee member was assigned to facilitate each pastor's and staff person's review. They used a typical business style review form and asked several people from the congregation to "anonymously" review the pastor's and/or staff person's performance. The problem with this is that neither the pastors nor the staff knew who was evaluating their performance. So, even if they received a positive review, it felt strange and unproductive. It felt like management through mysterious triangulation. The nature of the review depended on the people who got asked to do it, and you were not even allowed to know who they were. The problem with this type of performance review is that church leaders were trying to represent others instead of speaking directly on their own behalf.

We have shifted our review process to a far more direct approach. Our committee now works on the overall ministry review and the individual reviews together. In the overall ministry review, we look at how things are going in worship, discipleship, fellowship, and outreach. They meet together ahead of time and go over their preparation work for the overall and individual reviews. However, they meet with each pastor and staff person individually to go over their individual performance review. They deliver the overall ministry review in a meeting with the pastors and program staff together. The thing I like about this format is that it encourages honest feedback for the pastors and staff. The members of the Pastoral Relations Committee speak directly to us about their ideas and opinions. This process can be both encouraging and challenging, but it often leads into effective communication because the reviews are in no way anonymous. They are very direct and the communication is clear.

This review structure keeps the work environment feeling cooperative, rather than competitive. It emphasizes the fact that we are in it together. When the overall ministry is reviewed this has to do with the contributions of the pastors and staff, but also the volunteers. When the big picture is in front of you, then the focus is on what lies ahead congregationally. An overall ministry review can help your church to aim high with their eyes and to stay focused on what lies ahead. This has helped our review process to be filled with better conversations. Paying attention to the big picture helps a church to keep a proper perspective on all the other reviews. If things are going well in worship, discipleship, fellowship, and outreach, then the team and individuals should feel affirmed. If things are not going well in one or more of these areas, then everyone should feel challenged and, hopefully, the dialogue will lead to progress. The goal is always progress and improvements, not perfection or blame.

chapter 6

Community

The word *community* means different things to different people. However, it always has something to do with relationships. It is a set of relationships or a group of people with a clear source of identity or a clear set of boundaries. People often refer to the place where they live as a community. I live in a town called North Attleboro. This is one community to which I belong. The name of the town is our primary source of identity. People also refer to a sense of community within our churches. This has to do with the quality of the relationships that exist within a congregation. This kind of community is something we seek to develop through small study groups, fellowship activities, and friendships in the church. In this sense, community consists of the depth of relationships we have with others. Within the church, vulnerability is one thing that leads into our experience of community. I place community above creativity in the communication hierarchy because it takes more time to establish community than it does to make space for creativity. Trusted pastors are given permission to be creative long before a true sense of community has been established. The trust level has to deepen even further beyond the creative stage if a true sense of community is going to emerge. Developing community not only has to do with where a church is going, but also with how the church gets there and what the church people experience along the way.

Harmony

I was flying home from Chicago and waiting at my gate at O'Hare International Airport. Many of the passengers waiting to board the plane were already frustrated because we were delayed one hour. After the hour wait, we boarded the plane and eventually taxied out onto the tarmac. Then the engines on the plane shut down and the air stopped flowing. The pilot began to speak over the intercom. After introducing himself, he said, "I have good news and bad news." Then he said, "I will give you the bad news first." He said, "I have just been informed that we will have to wait another sixty minutes before we take off." The entire plane groaned loudly after hearing this. Then he said, "The good news is that I play the harmonica." Everyone laughed. Then the pilot actually started playing the harmonica. We laughed even harder. It was one of the funniest things I had ever experienced. After he finished his song, the pilot shut the lights off. No one was complaining or expressing their frustration. The people talked briefly with each other about this experience, then everyone went to sleep for the next hour.

One of the key components of developing community with each other has to do with taking ourselves less seriously and taking others more seriously. One sign of true community developing within your church is that you begin to laugh more often. The thing I love about the pilot with his harmonica is that he did not avoid the conflict situation. He shared the bad news quickly and directly. He then creatively used humor to encourage everyone to cooperate with the flight crew during this difficult situation. It was a great experience and a good example of a creative response. The laughter also led to an immediate sense of community on the plane. We were all frustrated by the delays, but the captain helped us to see that we were all in the same position. He helped us to see that we could not do anything about the delay, and that we should strive to make the best out of the situation. When we laughed together, it helped us to see that we not only shared the pain and the frustration, but also the joy and the laughter. This helped all of us to rest in the moment and release the anxiety.

In the past, I have struggled with the idea of focusing too much on avoiding triangulation as a way of being the church. On the surface, it did not seem particularly spiritual or biblical. I always saw the practice of avoiding triangles as administrative or systematic. Then, I started noticing how good Jesus was at avoiding triangles and how clearly he utilized direct communication. Jesus never played games in his relationships. His communication style was very direct. Jesus set a very clear example for us with love being in the center of all that he did. The basic premise of this book is that avoiding triangulation and utilizing direct communication will help churches to cultivate a clearer sense of community through love-filled relationships. We cannot force people to love one another, but we can encourage the spiritual practice of direct communication. This will inevitably help us to create an emotional environment in which love is amplified.

Relationships

D. Darrell Griffin compares a new pastor arriving to an established church with a person "arriving in the middle of a movie." He writes, "Newly appointed pastors enter into individual and collective congregational stories in progress."[1] How you listen to and come to understand the larger story of the congregation is a big part of the relationship that is being formed between a pastor and the congregation in this time of transition. Pastoral ministry is largely about building a relationship with the congregation you are serving. These relationships give shape to the story that is being written. Each chapter in a congregation's story is significant. The chapter you are currently writing with your church will have more significance if you understand that relationships rest at the center.

A colleague of mine from California recently shared an interesting story with me. One of the other local churches where he lived called a new senior pastor with a very established reputation. This new clergy person was a professor, author, and well-known Christian leader. However, he was never the pastor of a church. He was recently ordained in this denomination and was shifting from a life of teaching in the classroom to one of preaching and leading worship. This person's church welcomed him into town with a lot of fanfare. His reputation preceded him, and his congregation was filled with hope and expectation. My friend said that this new pastor came to an area clergy meeting a month after he arrived in this church and told the other clergy that he was surprised by the level of relational expectations people seemed to have. He said that he thought his new job was supposed to be about preaching and leading worship. Everyone in the room laughed. They laughed because they knew that the majority of the effort they put into ministry was about relationships, not performance in the pulpit. This pastor's reputation may have preceded him, but the glow of his reputation quickly faded. His ministry did not last a year. When a pastor fails to see that his or her role has a lot to do with relationships, this can have devastating results regardless of the pastor's credentials and reputation.

1. Griffin, *Transition Zone*, 5.

People like well-crafted sermons and effective worship leading, but at the end of the day, they are more concerned with a pastor's integrity, the integrity of the relationships they share with their pastor, and the integrity of the relationships the pastor has with the congregation as a whole. In a new church that is just being planted, you will write the first chapter in a larger story for a congregation. In an established church with a long history, many chapters have been written before you arrive, and they will continue to be written after you leave. A church is not a blank slate. The reason we are called to navigate the nonsense has to do with prioritizing mission and relationships. It has to do with keeping the purpose of the church alive for the congregations we serve. The purpose of the church is obviously not just to avoid triangulation. The purpose of the church is related to God's love and the great commandments. It is loving God with everything we have and loving our neighbor as ourselves.

I once heard a presentation by Craig Groeschel, the founding pastor of Life Church centered in Edmond, Oklahoma. This is a megachurch with multiple sites and tens of thousands of people. Craig was speaking at the Midwinter Conference of the Evangelical Covenant Church. Craig said that even though their church was over 50,000 people and had multiple sites, they still hold a philosophy that every person who becomes a part of our church ought to feel "known and needed." This megachurch pastor recognized that relationships within the church matter, even if he could not be in a relationship with every individual. None of us can have an emotionally intimate relationship with every member of our congregation, but within the confines of our personal and vocational limits, we need to do our best to show people that we care about them and the congregation as a whole.

Tenure

Many of the churches that call new pastors directly from the seminary have struggled with conflict and finding a way out of the basement of communication. At the time of her call, one pastor was twenty-six years old, right out of seminary, and in her first church as a lead pastor. The church she was in had a reputation for high-level conflict and difficulty in its relationship with pastors. She is one of the first pastors I directly encouraged to see her first three years of ministry as the "trust verses mistrust" stage. I suggested that these three years would be challenging, but that her life and relationship with the church would get better if she stuck with it and made it through these years. She is now in her fifth year of ministry, and I asked her how things are going. She explained that after the third year, she was able to claim her pastoral authority. She could now say and do things that she never felt comfortable doing during her first three years. She is now more proactive than reactive in ministry, and she said it is more fun.

This pastor was grateful to move beyond the tentativeness that existed in her relationships with people during these first three years. During the first three years of her ministry, people would say things like, "I have never heard a bad thing about you." It was hard for her to live under the perfect image people had of her. When someone finally got upset with her and left the church, it gave her some space to breathe and be herself again. There can be a false energy that exists within a congregation during these three years. This is why some pastors refer to this stage as the honeymoon. In this stage, pastors rely on the authority that is given to them because they are in the position. If you make it past the "trust verses mistrust" stage, then you rely more on the authority that you have earned. Trust can be a hard thing to establish, and yet it must be the goal for everyone involved in the first three years.

My first Conference Superintendent was a man named George Elia, and in my first few years of ministry, he encouraged me to stay in my churches long enough to "enjoy the fruits of my labor." It was a great piece of advice. He said that looking back on his ministries, he wished that he would have stayed a little longer in each place. Creativity and community take time to develop. They emerge from church cultures with high levels of trust and communication. When the church works well together, relationships develop more completely. Creativity has a lot to do with what the church is striving to do; whereas, the community that develops has to do with who the church is becoming. When a new pastor is leading a congregation, it can take four or five years before creativity begins to emerge. However, it can take up to six or seven years to develop a clear sense of community with your congregation. If a pastor leaves before the first three years are completed, then the people in the congregation will say it was not a good fit. If a pastor leaves in the five- to seven-year range, then the congregation can feel like they were used as a stepping stone. When a pastor reaches the ten- to twelve-year mark, then the congregation experiences the sense that they have completed a chapter.

Opportunities

In Eugene Peterson's book *Under the Unpredictable Plant*, he writes about pastors taking "a vow of stability." He says there is nothing wrong with looking for or accepting another call. However, "Far too many pastors change parishes out of adolescent boredom, not as a consequence of mature wisdom."[2] Many pastors experience a seven-year itch. They get beyond the trust verses mistrust stage. They survive the first three years, and then they serve faithfully for several more years. These years tend to be productive, and people can be recognized for their strength of leadership in this period. This can lead to phone calls coming from denominational leaders and other potential churches. This feels affirming and there can be some anxiety about missing opportunities that are set before us. Often, though, pastors do not pay enough attention to their current situations, and it is here that I would like to see clergy ask if they are finished writing the current chapter. Stability in a pastorate may lead pastors to places they cannot go spiritually and communally if they move on to a new place. One sign that a true sense of community is developing is that church members will begin sharing their stories more completely. After community is established pastors are often given access to the deepest places and the darkest corners in people's lives. This work can be transformative. So pastors ought to ask if the work they were called to in this location is finished.

Sometimes I think we confuse opportunity with call. Just because there are new opportunities does not mean that you are being called to them. One good question you can ask yourself is, "Have I stayed long enough to enjoy the fruits of my labor?" The fruit of your labor is the true sense of community you begin to experience after you have been in a church beyond six or seven years. There is nothing wrong with seeing how one experience is connected to the next in the call process. My only concern is related to the level of commitment that we have to finishing what we have started. Larger congregations also tend to have bigger challenges. Sometimes if you move too soon these challenges can become overwhelming in your next place. This is why we need to discern the difference between an opportunity and a call. We need to ask ourselves if we truly prepared for the new challenges that will come in these new locations.

I am not saying that the ministry of a pastor is only significant if she stays beyond ten years. I am simply saying that this typically represents a

2. Peterson, *Unpredictable Plant*, 29.

full chapter in the life of a church. Significant ministry can take place in the first few days or weeks of a ministry. People do experience change and transformation through the things that are said, done, and experienced in the midst of a transition period. However, it would be shortsighted if we fail to see the impact that length of stay can have for congregations. Something significant happens after three years in terms of your ability to be creative. You are able to be more adventurous and experimental. Your congregation is more willing to try new things. It is like a switch is flicked on after you finish your third year. Then it is as if the light that was switched on has a dimmer lever, and you spend the next few years moving the dimmer switch up, so that the light can shine brighter, because even more significant things happen after five or six years with regard to establishing community within your congregation.

A retired pastor in our denomination once told me that he heard the late Robert Schuller speak at a conference about longevity in ministry. He said that Schuller's theory was that most pastors do not stay long enough, because their canvases are too small. When artists begin a painting, they first select the size of the canvas they will use for their artwork. Schuller suggested that we would all stay longer in our churches if we had a larger canvas, or a broader vision in mind for what God might help us to accomplish through our work in a particular congregation. One friend of mine just finished his fifteenth year of ministry. He clearly feels like he has finished writing a chapter in the life of this congregations, but we also talked extensively about his desire to stay in this location for another chapter. I noticed that he had a clear call toward this next chapter in the life of his church. Rediscovering this sense of call and recasting a vision were essential before he could recommit fully to this congregation. This is why the twenty-year scenario is such an effective tool. It helps us to see beyond our current circumstances and to expand the canvas with regard to our long-term vision.

Redemption

One great example of someone in need of re-visioning is Peter after Jesus' death and resurrection. As predicted Peter had denied Jesus three times before the crucifixion, and there was clearly a significant amount of unresolved brokenness between them. Jesus was concerned about how these unresolved issues might impact Peter's ministry in the long run. In John 21:15-17 it says,

> When they had finished breakfast, Jesus said to Simon Peter, "Simon son of John, do you love me more than these?" Peter said to him, "Yes, Lord; you know that I love you." Jesus said to him, "Feed my lambs." A second time he said to him, "Simon son of John, do you love me?" He said to him, "Yes, Lord; you know that I love you." Jesus said to him, "Tend my sheep." He said to him the third time, "Simon son of John, do you love me?" Peter felt hurt because he said to him the third time, "Do you love me?" And Peter said to him, "Lord you know everything; you know that I love you." Jesus said to him, "Feed my sheep."

It is really important here to notice that Jesus was not avoiding the issue that existed between them. Peter had denied Jesus three times and so Jesus asked Peter the question, "Do you love me?" three times. He asked Peter this question until it hurt because he was trying to repair their relationship.

This story is a powerful example of just how direct of a communicator Jesus was. He went right to the heart of the matter and did not avoid this difficult subject. This is an important lesson for all church leaders. We need to be willing to talk about the difficult things that need our attention. The key is learning how to address these matters honestly and lovingly at the same time. Pain is something we all have to deal with in life, and there is a difference between judging someone and confronting an issue. Most of the time, we want to avoid difficult conversations with people who we have hurt or who have hurt us in some way. These can be painful and complicated conversations, but they are worth having. The reason we embrace direct communication is to reveal the love of Christ to one another inside Christian community. The key to developing a culture of direct communication within your church system is being able to say that this is how we do things here.

Revival

True Christian community is related to developing a church culture in which your ministries are allowed to function and flourish. It has to do with your church developing more creativity and community. With this in mind, churches do not need more micromanagers; they need macromanagers. Micromanagers try to control everything that takes place within their churches. These are leaders who want to be in control of everything and everyone. They are always afraid that something may go wrong. Macro-managers see the big picture, and they help to reveal a broad vision to their congregations. They understand why the church exists, and they have strong convictions about how the church ought to fulfill this purpose. They are willing to go on adventures or to launch congregational experiments. When pastors become macro-managers, they guide their congregations into the future without controlling all the details. They encourage the people of the church to be involved in their ministries and with the future of their congregations. They empower their congregations by equipping the saints to do the work of the ministry.

One joy-filled example of our church being willing to take a risk is an experience I had with a high school student in Attleboro. I helped this student set up a pre-college internship for her senior year. This student sensed a call to study youth ministry in college. She was an energetic leader in our church, and had already been using her time and talents in the realms of youth ministry and music ministry. She helped one Friday a month with our Explorers Youth Group for third, fourth, and fifth graders. She helped with our Sunday school music program, and she had played an active role in our drama ministry. She came to me at the end of her junior year and said that she wanted more responsibility in the church. I had the clear sense that she already had plenty of responsibility, but what she really wanted was more authority. I figured that the best way to do this was to have her do an internship so that I could share authority with her in an official way.

Our church was planning on starting a new youth group called Pathfinders for students in kindergarten and the first and second grades. I asked Hayley if she would like to be fully responsible for this program, and she agreed to it. Pathfinders met on the first Wednesday of every month. I asked Hayley to develop a theme for each month and to begin planning the curriculum around these themes. She also worked out the schedule and invited adult leaders to be involved. I already planned on being a part of this new ministry, so I attended most of these events, but I contributed only when Hayley asked me to do something. She was not only given responsibility, but also authority in this situation. She did a great job with the program. She made some wise decisions along the way. She also learned valuable lessons. This all helped her to develop a successful new program for our church. The children involved with this program were thrilled to be there. This group included young people from our church and the community.

It was an outreach that clearly has had an impact. This program had an impact on these students and on this emerging young leader.

When churches are thriving and experiencing a profound level of community, great things happen. Ministry opportunities appear and are acted upon by your church members. Relationships grow stronger, and conflicts are resolved more quickly and with integrity. Church leaders work together to face challenges and to take advantage of ministry opportunities. Appropriate risks are taken to help the church fulfill its mission, and church staff and volunteer leaders work cooperatively, collaboratively, and creatively. On occasion, there are relational experiences that give you a glimpse of the way things are going to be when God ushers in a new heaven and a new earth. We live in a chaotic world, where things are not as they should be. However, when the church is truly being the church, and we are all striving first for God's kingdom, then we begin to experience life as it eventually will be. We experience God's hand in the midst of our ministries, and we see God's fingerprints on the things we are experiencing. This kind of Christian community allows us to proceed confidently, knowing that "The Lord will keep our going out and our coming in from this time on and forever more" (Ps 121:8).

Best Practice #6

Congregational Discernment

There is a leadership theory that "It is easier to ask for forgiveness than it is to ask for permission." Leaders who employ this philosophy see that they can make decisions quickly for their churches and deal with the consequences after the fact. This kind of approach is why many pastors fail the trust verses mistrust stage in their first three years. They get their way without having to ask permission, but they also lose their way and the trust needed to be truly accepted as a leader. There is nothing wrong with apologizing after you do something wrong, but people will lose trust in your leadership if they perceive you are following this pattern on purpose. Sometimes the changes we make in this way last, but they are often unsupported. So you get your way initially, but these changes rarely have the impact you hope they will have. This type of decision-making keeps the people in your church from trusting your leadership. A Presbyterian pastor told me that he rearranged a set of pews in his sanctuary at his church without any conversation. During his first vacation the building and grounds committee moved them back and bolted them firmly in place.

My philosophy is that it is always better to ask for permission than it is for forgiveness. This is why congregational discernment on all difficult decisions is a good path to follow. Allowing others to be a part of these discussions helps them to embrace the decisions and to feel a part of the direction the congregation is taking. Some of the decisions we make congregationally are merely a matter of human preference. I do not think the color of carpeting in you fellowship hall is God's big priority. When picking colors you are merely finding out the will of the majority. But in matters that are central to the mission of the church, it is always helpful to remind your church that the will of God is what you are after. In these matters, we are not merely trying to figure out the preferable way, the easiest way, the least expensive way, or even the highest-quality way. In these matters we are trying to figure out God's way in accordance with our kingdom responsibilities and the missional impact of our decisions. If you avoid discernment on this level you will keep ministry dreams buried because of fear. If you do this then the church will never grow and thrive. Avoiding important conversations is a surefire roadblock to momentum.

When we make major decisions congregationally, our ministries are given the opportunity to prosper. If important decisions are made congregationally, there is typically little if any conflict about the decision-making process. When churches make mission-minded decisions together, the people get behind those decisions, and they help their churches to fulfill the mission. One pastor I have been working with utilized this philosophy and his congregation was surprised by the number of unanimous votes they were experiencing. He said they were not used to congregational decision-making, but pleasantly surprised by how easy it was and also how meaningful it seemed to be. This kind of consensus about the direction a church is heading can lead into a tremendous amount of momentum. Some pastors and church leaders resist this kind of decision-making because it takes some of the power away from the staff or the central board. My experience has been that it empowers the congregation and enables you to establish momentum.

When you wait until issues become controversial before you use congregational decision-making, it makes congregational decision-making look bad. The establishment of your annual budget is one task that requires congregational discernment. This is a task which receives congregational attention each and every year in most churches. We do it this way because it is a matter of establishing priorities and direction for the church. Managing the budgeting process is the responsibility of our governing body. The governing body of your church is charged with finding a balance between fiscal responsibility and the vision of your congregation. This group receives input from our staff, boards, and ministry teams. Then this group establishes the final budget and presents it to the congregation for approval. It is a major mistake for any group in the church to look at budgeting only in terms of fiscal responsibility. In other words, this is not a job for the finance committee alone.

The reason you need congregational input toward your budget is to make sure this balance between vision and responsibility is maintained. If you have a governing body in a triangle with a finance committee or the trustees, this process will always be difficult. Discernment is important in our churches because churches need to figure out what their priorities are. The truth of the matter is that most clergy and staff know that there are limited resources. At the same time, it is important to discern priorities together to establish goals and a vision which gives the community a sense of enthusiasm. If the people of the church know that there are plans to move the ministries forward but there is a lack of resources to make this happen, then you may be surprised to see new levels of giving. High levels of morale and enthusiasm often lead to significant increases in the realms of stewardship and vision.

When a church calls a pastor in our denomination, the governing body typically appoints a search committee, and the search committee is approved by the congregation. The search committee reviews resumes and profiles of potential pastors. Some of these candidates are interviewed by the committee, and one candidate is presented to the congregation. The congregation typically meets this candidate, listens to him or her preach, asks questions, and then votes on the candidate. This kind of search process reveals how our major decisions can be shared by congregations and their leaders. In this case the governing body selects a diverse group of people to represent the church and find a candidate, but they give the final step of discernment over to the congregation. Congregational discernment is an important practice for most churches. Even in churches without congregational polity there are ways to include your congregations in the major decisions that are made. The goal is sharing both authority and responsibility with our congregations. It is to develop as much cooperation, collaboration, creativity, and community as we possibly can. This is a call to expand God's impact on our churches, communities, and world.

Ministry Repercussions

In 2 Corinthians 5:18-20, it says that God was "reconciling the world to himself" and that through Christ he is "entrusting the message of reconciliation to us." The reason God is in the process of "reconciling the world to himself" is because there is a very clear gap between the way things are and the way things ought to be. There is a gap between the way we are and the way we should be. There is also a gap between the way the church is and the way it ought to be. Finally, there is a gap between the way our world is and the way it should be. Our call to stand in the gap as "ambassadors for Christ" is a broad vision for the church. It is a vision entrusted to his disciples. Now God wants us to buy into this vision as well, and this is why he wants us to take our ministries seriously. Through this passage the Apostle Paul reveals that Jesus is involved with a giant restoration project. He is trying to restore our lives, our families, our churches, our communities, our nation, and our world simultaneously. He also wants us to be a part of this restoration project as well. This is why he has entrusted us with this ministry of reconciliation. Jesus wants us to stand in this gap between the way things are and the way they ought to be.

There are three primary ways people approach worship each Sunday morning that have an impact on our ability to stand in this gap. People go to church either feeling righteous, religious, or reunited. When you go to worship feeling *righteous*, then you look around at other people in your neighborhood on your way to church and you convince yourself that you are better than they are because you are going to church, and they are not. You may even arrive in the sanctuary and look around and convince yourself that you are better than the other people around you. Maybe you are more committed, devoted, or disciplined than others. Another way to approach worship on a Sunday morning is feeling *religious*. This is the emotional response to doing your duty or fulfilling an obligation. You go to church with a virtual time card in your heart. You punch the virtual time clock when you arrive. You go to worship either because you have to, or ought to, not because you want to.

The final way to attend worship on a Sunday morning is feeling *reunited.* You attend worship because when you do you feel reunited with God and God's people. Worship is seen as an opportunity, not an obligation. Gathering together in the presence of Christ has to do with standing together in God's grace. Worship attendance is not about a proud posture of self-righteousness. It is not about fulfilling our religious obligations or making ourselves look good. It's about joining with others in a shared experience of the good news. It's about laying down your sin and pain before God and receiving his love and acceptance. It's about acknowledging your brokenness with others and offering the same grace we hope to receive from them. When we approach worship feeling reunited, then we see every Sunday morning as a celebration of God's grace. These celebrations end up being the fertile soil in which true Christian faith and Christ-centered community develop. When we approach worship in this way our focus is on the relationships we have with God and each other.

The good news we discover is that God's plans are bigger than our mistakes and his purpose is broader than our sins or our brokenness. This is why navigating the nonsense is so important. If we improve our communication patterns within the church, then we will do a better job of staying out of God's way and staying focused on what God wants us to accomplish. Some people believe they have all the answers in terms of what we need to do to improve our lives and our churches. Conservative Christians think that the church simply needs to become more conservative. Liberal Christians think that the church needs to become more liberal. I do not think any sector of the church has a corner on what is wrong with us. I think our issues run deeper than this and that there are opportunities for all of us to experience the restorative work that Christ wants to accomplish in our lives and our churches.

God wants us to see our worship experiences as a reunion each Sunday. God wants us to enjoy the diversity within our congregations. God wants our experience of the Christian faith and Christian community to be a celebration. There is a reason we call the gospel good news. When we gather together for worship, it is an opportunity for us to connect with God and God's people. We set aside the disconnectedness of our human experience and shallow interactions, and we embrace the interconnectedness of our Christian faith and fellowship. We dive into the deep end of what God has in mind for us. We experience the depths of what God is up to in our world. Navigating the nonsense helps us to stand in this gap and to stay out of God's way. Direct communication helps us to deepen our relationships and to refine our focus on his will. Getting out of the basement and pursuing the higher elevations through the hard work of cooperation and collaboration enables healthy community and high levels of creativity for the sake of the gospel. This is where God would like to see all of our churches. May the Father, the Son, and the Holy Spirit bless all of you and your congregations on these amazing journeys.

Benediction

"Come to him, a living stone, though rejected by mortals yet chosen and precious in God's sight, and like living stones, let yourselves be built into a spiritual house, to be a holy priesthood, to offer spiritual sacrifices acceptable to God through Jesus Christ" (1 Pet 2:4–5).

Bibliography

Augsburger, David. *Caring Enough to Confront: How to Understand and Express Your Deepest Feelings Toward Others*. Grand Rapids: Revell, 2009.

Barton, Ruth Haley. *Pursuing God's Will Together: A Discernment Practice for Leadership Groups*. Downers Grove, IL: InterVarsity, 2012.

Bixby, Douglas. *Challenging the Church Monster: From Conflict to Community*. Eugene, OR: Wipf and Stock, 2007.

Friedman, Edwin. *A Failure of Nerve: Leadership in the Age of the Quick Fix*. New York: Church Publishing, 2007.

Griffin, D. Darrell. *Navigating Pastoral Leadership in the Transition Zone: Arriving in the Middle of the Movie*. Chicago: MMGI, 2012.

Hotchkiss, Dan. *Governance and Ministry: Rethinking Board Leadership*. Herndon, VA: Alban, 2009.

Kouzes, Jim, and Barry Posner. *A Leader's Legacy*. San Francisco: Jossey-Bass, 2006.

Kroeger, Otto, and Janet Thuesen. *Type Talk: The 16 Personality Types That Determine How We Live, Love, and Work*. New York: Dell, 1988.

Lencioni, Patrick. *The Five Dysfunctions of a Team: A Leadership Fable*. San Francisco: Jossey-Bass, 2002.

McManus, Erwin Raphael. *An Unstoppable Force: Daring to Become the Church God Had in Mind*. Loveland, CO: Group, 2001.

Nixon, Paul. *I Refuse to Lead a Dying Church!* Cleveland: Pilgrim, 2006.

Papalia, Diane, and Sally Wendkos Olds. *Human Development*. New York: McGraw-Hill, 1986.

Peterson, Eugene. *Under the Unpredictable Plant: An Exploration in Vocational Holiness*. Grand Rapids: Eerdmans, 1992.

Rendle, Gill, and Susan Beaumont. *When Moses Meets Aaron: Staffing and Supervision in Large Congregations*. Herndon, VA: Alban, 2007.

Ruth, Kibbie Simmons, and Karen McClintock. *Healthy Disclosure: Solving Communication Quandaries in Congregations*. Herndon, VA: Alban, 2007.

Steinke, Peter. *Congregational Leadership in Anxious Times: Being Calm and Courageous No Matter What*. Herndon, VA: Alban, 2006.

———. *Healthy Congregations: A Systems Approach*. Herndon, VA: Alban, 2006.